Robert Campbell

A Pilgrimage to my Motherland

An Account of a Journey Among the Egbas and Yorubas of Central Africa

Robert Campbell

A Pilgrimage to my Motherland

An Account of a Journey Among the Egbas and Yorubas of Central Africa

ISBN/EAN: 9783337011147

Printed in Europe, USA, Canada, Australia, Japan

Cover: Foto ©Andreas Hilbeck / pixelio.de

More available books at **www.hansebooks.com**

A Pilgrimage to My Motherland.

AN

ACCOUNT OF A JOURNEY

AMONG

THE EGBAS AND YORUBAS OF CENTRAL AFRICA,

In 1859-60.

BY

ROBERT CAMPBELL,

One of the Commissioners of the Niger Valley Exploring Party; late in charge of the Scientific Department of the Institute for Colored Youth, Philadelphia; and Member of the International Statistical Congress, London.

New-York:
PUBLISHED BY THOMAS HAMILTON, 48 BEEKMAN ST.
PHILADELPHIA:
BY THE AUTHOR, 661 NORTH THIRTEENTH ST.

1861.

ENTERED, according to Act of Congress, in the year 1860, by
ROBERT CAMPBELL,
In the Clerk's Office of the District Court of the United States, for the Southern District of New-York.

DEDICATION.

To those friends in America and in England who generously contributed to the expense of the expedition, one of the objects of which was to make the observations and obtain the facts recorded in the following pages; but particularly to BENJAMIN COATES, of Philadelphia, whose unremitting efforts contributed in no small degree to the success of the enterprise, and to HENRY CHRISTY, of London, to whom chiefly the friends of Africa and the Negro are indebted for the co-operation of the English people, this little narrative is respectfully dedicated by

THE AUTHOR.

ADVERTISEMENT.

ALTHOUGH it is desired that this little volume should be sold entirely on its own merits, yet the friends of Christian Civilization in Africa are informed, that the profits are intended to aid the author in defraying the expense of removing with his family to Abbeokuta, which place he has adopted as his future home.

PREFACE.

THE intention was to prepare only a small pamphlet, containing those points of general information respecting the Egbas and Yorubas, as persons interested in the objects of my visit to those people would wish to learn; but in spite of efforts to be brief, the work has attained its present dimensions, with the length of which, however, as a book, there is certainly no cause of complaint. The narrative is, as far as possible, confined to personal observations, though this has perhaps deprived the casual reader of some details otherwise interesting. Much error, particularly in reference to Africa, has been propagated in consequence of writers generally not confining the subject of their books to their own observations. In my own case, I presume, the sources of information being equally accessible, that the intelligent reader can obtain for himself, as easily as I can for him, whatever information he desires about the early history of Africa, its ancient races, and the efforts of the Portuguese, British and Dutch to circumnavigate and colonize the continent.

Several items of information are omitted, partly because they are not of general interest, and partly because my worthy colleague and brother, Dr. M. R. Delany, will include them in the Report of our Expedition, the labor of which he has kindly assumed.

After what is written in the context, if I am still asked what I think of Africa for a colored man to live and do well in, I simply answer, that with as good prospects in America as colored men generally, I have determined, with my wife and children, to go to Africa to live, leaving the inquirer to interpret the reply for himself. R. C.

CONTENTS.

CHAPTER I.
LIVERPOOL TO LAGOS.
Bathurst—Sierra Leone—Malignant Fever—Cape Palmas—Cape Coast Castle—Acra, English and Dutch, ... 9

CHAPTER II.
ARRIVAL AT LAGOS.
Bad bar—Landing mails under difficulties—Magnificent Spectacle—Dexterous Canoemen—Offering to the Water-demon—Sharks—Mr. Turner—The Consulate—Lieut. Lodder—Disgusting Spectacle—Lagos—Alcoholic Stimulants and Fever—Emigrants—Cowries—King Docemo—Kosoko, ex-king—A Visit to the Palace—Unfortunate Adventure—The Lesson, ... 14

CHAPTER III.
JOURNEY TO ABBEOKUTA.
The Crowthers—River Ogun—Ogboi Creek—Nymphæa—Rhizophora Mangle—Villages in the Swamp—Steam Navigation on the Ogun—Fish-Snares—Current—Rocky Bed—Crossing on Calabashes—"Agayen"—Subterranean Streams—Aro—Orange Cottage, ... 25

CHAPTER IV.
ABBEOKUTA.
Introduction to the "Alake"—Royal Attire—Wives, over one hundred—Ogboni Elders—Native Game, *Wari*—Visit to the Chiefs, ... 28

CHAPTER V
NATIVE AUTHORITIES.
Peculiarity of Government—"Ibashorun" or Prime Minister—Shukenu—"His Highness Ogubonna," Friend of Civilization—"You are of my own Kindred"—Atambala—Age—Mr. Crowther and the Doctors—Order of Succession—Departments of Government—Shodeke, ... 36

CHAPTER VI.
MISCELLANEOUS.
African Cities—Forms of "Compounds"—Native Food—Clothing—Industry—Percolator—Blacksmiths—Iron-smelting—Weaving—Farming Implements Indigo—Palm-oil Factories—"Taffi"—Traders—Personal Habits—Cola-nuts—Native Affability—Onoshoko, "Father of the King"—Polygamy—Slavery—African Honor—Symmetry of Form—Calisthenics—Archery—Native Games of Skill—Stray Fact—Wild Bees—An Adventure—Funeral—Processions—Discovery of Abbeokuta, ... 43

CHAPTER VII.
RELIGION.

Shango exorcised—Existence of Spirits—Ifa—Agugu—Oro—Aspect of a City on Oro-day—Gymnastic Sports—Pugilistic Encounters—Missions,......... 74

CHAPTER VIII.
JOURNEY TO YORUBA.

Our Caravan—Atadi—Extortion of Carriers—Ilugun—Peter Elba—Open Air Accommodation—Articles left by the roadside for sale—Ijaye—Kumi—Telegraphic Drums—Interview with Chief—"Palaver with the water"—Great Market—The Drivers—Carriers—Value of a Shirt—Departure for Oyo—Fever Again—Visit to King Adelu—Exchange of Presents—Tax collecting—Snake-Charmer—Adeneji—Small Pox—Ogbomishaw—Dr. Delany, Fever still again—Scarcity of Water,..................................... 82

CHAPTER IX.
ILORIN.

Magnificent Conflagration—Grassy Plains and Forests—Freedom of the Country from Beasts and Reptiles; why—Extravagant Welcome—Nasamo the Executioner, and his Dwelling—Wifeless—Royal Present of Food—Prisoners—Interview with the King—Schools—Arahians—Mulatto—Musical Instruments—Banjo—Beggars—Looms—Gambari Market—Escort, ...:... 99

CHAPTER X.
RETURN.

"Two Horsemen," and their Adventure—Exchange Horses—What about Vaughn—Progress Arrested—New Route—Voices in the Bush—Village in Ashes—Isehin—A Hunting Party—Dead Man by the Roadside—Ibadan Soldiers, another Adventure—"Enough, Enough, white man, go on!"—A City on a Hill—Berecadu, and its Defenses—Night Travel in Africa—Abbeokuta again—"The Dahomians are Coming"—Deputation—The Doctor is come, and how he did it—Final Departure for the Coast—The Carrier Nuisance once more—Troubles—Heroic Woman—Safe at Lagos—Departure—Kru men—A Slaver,... 108

CHAPTER XI
CONCLUSION.

Willingness of Natives to receive Settlers—Comparative Healthiness of Coast and Interior—Expense of Voyage—Protection—How to procure Land—Commercial and Agricultural Prospects—Time of Arriving at Lagos—The Bar—Extent of Self-Government—Climate—African Fever and Treatment—Cotton Trade—Domestic Animals—Agricultural Products—Minerals—Timber—Water—African Industry—Expense of Labor—Our Treaty—*Finis*,.. 184

A Pilgrimage to My Motherland.

CHAPTER I.

LIVERPOOL TO LAGOS.

Bathurst—Sierra Leone—Malignant Fever—Cape Palmas—Cape Coast Castle—Acra, English and Dutch.

ON the 24th June, 1859, I departed from Liverpool on board the African S. S. "Ethiope," Capt. French. On the 2d of July we arrived at Funchal, Madeira; the 4th was spent at Santa Cruz, Teneriffe, four days after leaving which we came in sight of Cape Verde, Africa; the next day we anchored in the port of Bathurst on the Gambia. This little town is built on one of those great deposits of sand commonly found on the Deltas of large rivers. It is said to be surrounded by very unhealthy influences, although the American Consul, with whom I enjoyed an hour's conversation, assured me that he had not known a case of fever among the white inhabitants of the place for six months. The trade is chiefly in ground-nuts, (*Arachis Hypogea.*) Except perhaps Freetown, there is not a better looking place on the West Coast. The largest houses are built along the river-side, and present a handsome appearance, heightened by some fine large trees growing before them, and a fine avenue is left between the trees and houses. The streets are wide and regularly intersect at right angles, with sewers for draining; the town, which from being low would otherwise be swampy, is thus kept dry. The white inhabitants, including the officers of the garrison and the missionaries, comprise about thirty persons. There is another small town about one hundred and fifty miles up the Gambia, called Macarthy's Island. The settlements on this river are British, and are garrisoned by African soldiers from the W I. Regiment. The natives are chiefly Jolofs and Mandingas. Many of the latter, who are Mohammedans, read and write Arabic; both comprise some very active and successful traders.

On the 12th we were at anchor in the harbor of Freetown, Sierra Leone, lat. 8° 29′ N., long. 13° 14′ W., said to be the best harbor on the West Coast of Africa. Affairs were in a bad condition, the yellow fever, or as some say, a malignant form of bilious fever had appeared there, and swept off more than a third of the white inhabitants, while the small pox was busy among the natives. During the two days that the ship continued in the port I had frequent opportunities of conversing with several of the natives, men of respectability, and in some instances of education; they complain bitterly of some of the Europeans, on account of their laxity of morals and unblushing disregard of the demands of decency. It is fortunate that the number of this class of persons is small compared with the number of high-minded, worthy men who are deservedly much esteemed.

On the 17th, Sunday, we arrived at Cape Palmas. Our stay there was short. I contrived to spend about three hours on shore, and was fortunate in meeting the Reverend Alex. Crummell, who conducted me to the two or three places of interest which could be visited in that time; amongst the rest he took me to the church in which he sometimes officiates. I was much gratified to witness more than one hundred natives, including an old chief, listening with deep attention to the word of God. I regret exceedingly not being able to accompany my Reverend friend to Mount Vaughn, his school and dwelling a little way from the town, where he is doing efficient service in training some promising native boys, a few of whom I met in his company. Here I received intelligence of the arrival of the barque "Mendi" at Monrovia, with my colleague Dr. Delany on board.

On the 19th July we arrived off Cape Coast Castle,

situated in lat. 5° 6′, N., long. 1° 5′ W. The town is not so low as either Bathurst or Lagos, but at the same time not more healthy than either. It was originally founded by the Portuguese; the British became its owners in 1672. The immediate site of the town wears a very rugged and barren aspect, but there are some beautiful green hills in the background where Indian corn and other products are cultivated. Gold dust is the principal article of export—the gold is chiefly brought from the Ashantee country in the interior, but the women procure small quantities after rain by washing the black sand scraped from the sea-beach and water-courses. The landing is bad, although the native canoe-men manage so well as seldom to wet their passengers. The inhabitants experience great want of water, relying for their supply on wells and pools which are frequently dry, and the latter sometimes muddy and unwholesome. The natives are very industrious, and manufacture tolerably fine articles of jewelry. The women both of this place and of Acra wear a strange-looking appendage to their dress immediately at the base of the lumbar region. Bustle would be hardly an appropriate term for it, as, although worn in about the same position, the appearance is different; and though used as a support for infants, which African women universally carry on their backs, it is evidently not intended solely for that purpose, as the women in other sections of Africa carry their children without such support, and many use it who have no children to carry. The women are generally very tastefully attired, displaying about their persons many trinkets of pure gold.

Early in the morning of the 20th we found ourselves anchored in the roads off Acra. This place is remarkable for being both British and Dutch; it is in fact simply two forts, one owned by each party, and the people's allegiance being thus divided, there is considerable confusion in collecting taxes, etc. There were some disturbances at the time of my visit, growing out of this cause.

CHAPTER II.

ARRIVAL AT LAGOS.

Bad bar—Landing mail under difficulties—Magnificent Spectacle—Dexterous Canoe-men—Offering to the Water-demon—Sharks—Mr. Turner—The Consulate, Lieut. Lodder—Disgusting Spectacle—Lagos—Alcoholic Stimulants and Fever—Emigrants—Cowries—King Docemo—Kosoko, ex-King—A Visit to the Palace—Unfortunate Adventure—The Lesson.

On the 21st July, early in the afternoon, our ship anchored off Lagos.

Our arrival was at the most unpropitious season of the year, the bar being then and during all June, July, and August more dangerous than at any other time; we found it impossible to effect any communication except by signals. The next day some natives were persuaded to come off from the beach; the bar being still very unsafe, they carried off the mails secured in a cask, and I, leaving my packages in charge of a man who accompanied me from Manchester, ventured to go on shore in their boat, which, however, I would not have done had I been aware of the great risk I incurred.

Could one but have divested himself of the sense of

danger, the scene was magnificent—the huge " swells " chasing each other, and our little bark now riding victoriously on the crest of one, then engulfed in a deep chasm between two others, rising high on both sides. It is perhaps impossible for men to evince more dexterity than these natives in the control of their canoes, especially on approaching the beach. There were twelve men paddling with two others, one steering and the other in the prow watching the approaching surges and directing accordingly. When near the beach, the last, who is their head man, with much ceremony pours a few drops of rum on the water, and a great deal more down his throat, after which he very vehemently harangues, first I suppose the demon of the water to whom the rum was offered, and then his crew, cheering them for their work. There was another native on the beach who gave directions of some sort to the steersman by strange gesticulations; his appearance, as he stood above a group of companions, himself mounted on an inverted surf-boat with his loose garments waving in the air, presented a subject which would have delighted an artist, and was indeed wildly picturesque. It is necessary to watch carefully the regular successive rise and fall of the waves in order to prevent them breaking over the boat. Within a few yards of the beach they stop, "backing water" and watching intently their leader, then at a signal from him, they dash on vigorously on the top of a wave. As soon as the canoe touches, simultaneously they are in the water, and seizing their frail craft, in an instant bear her high and dry on the beach.

The bar of Lagos is dangerous chiefly on account of the large number of sharks which are always ready to make a repast on the bodies of the unfortunate occupants of any boat capsizing there.

The difficulties of the bar are not, however, insuperable: small vessels can always easily sail over it into the fine bay within, where they can load or unload with little trouble and without risk. It is not so easy to go out again, however, for then it would be necessary to "beat" against the wind; but a small steamboat could at once take them out in tow with perfect safety. I was informed that slavers used always to enter the bay: they could of course afford to wait for a favorable wind with which to get out. On landing I was kindly received by a Mr. Turner, a re-captured slave, educated at Sierra Leone by the British, and now a respectable merchant at Lagos.

After partaking of some refreshments provided by my hospitable friend, I was conducted to the house of Lieut. Lodder, the acting Consul, to whom I brought a letter from Lord Malmesbury, British Minister for Foreign Affairs in the late Derby Administration. My reception was cordial, and I was afforded convenient accommodation at the Consulate all the time I continued at Lagos.

A disgusting spectacle presented itself at the entrance of the river: on the right margin stood two bodies, transfixed by poles passing through their mouths. They were nearly dry, and strange to say were not disturbed by buzzards, although a great number of these birds—fortunately very abundant in Africa—were flying about them. They were two of five men who were executed for robbery: one of them was the son of a chief, and his connection with the party gave rise to a great "palaver," his friends contending that in consequence of his birth he should not suffer a malefactor's death, while others contended that his crime had degraded him to the position of other men, like whom he should answer for his offenses.

Lagos is a small island about six miles in circumference, located on the west coast of Africa, in the Bight of Benin, Gulf of Guinea, lat. 6° 24′ N., long. 3° 22′ E. Like Bathurst, on the Gambia, it is very low, and formed by an accumulation of sand. In some places lower than the surface of the river, it is very swampy from the infiltration of water. Like many localities on the coast of tropical countries, it is unhealthy. The prevailing disease is fever with chills: with common prudence, however, there is nothing to fear in this disease; but if the person suffering from it will blindly persist in the use of alcoholic stimulants, the consequence might be serious. I am sorry to say that Europeans and others, generally indulge far too freely in these beverages. In too many instances, I believe the climate is blamed for the evils thus created. After passing through what is called the acclimating process, which lasts during twelve or fifteen months, one is seldom troubled again with fever.

The population of Lagos is estimated at about thirty thousand: there are about fifteen hundred emigrants from Sierra Leone, the Brazils and Cuba. All these are themselves native Africans, brought from the interior and sold on different parts of the coast. Those from Sierra Leone are recaptured, and the others redeemed slaves. Few are more than half civilized. The white inhabitants number about twenty-five, and include English, Germans, French, Italians, and Portuguese. A few very fine houses have been erected near the water-side, and others were being built at the time of our departure. They use as money small shells (*Cypræa Moneta*) called cowries by the English, *owu* by the natives, this being also the general term for money. The value of the dollar and its fractions, as well as English currency, is well understood and appreciated: it is fast getting to be the same at Abbeokuta.

The present King of Lagos is called Docemo. He was placed in the position by the late Consul Campbell, after his brother Kosoko was deposed for warring against the English, and for his participation in the slave-trade. Kosoko has still a few adherents, particularly among the Europeans: only the guns of H. M. gun-boat "Brune," lying always in the river, preserve the present King his position. Kosoko lives not far from Lagos: he is said to be cruel and tyrannical, and still claims to be the legitimate King of the place.

On the morning of the first of August I made a visit to his Majesty King Docemo. Lieut. Lodder, the acting Consul, sent a messenger to his Majesty, informing him of the intended visit, and asking his permission, which being obtained, a party, consisting of the Commander of the "Brune," the Paymaster of H. M. S. S. "Medusa," the acting Consul and myself, proceeded. We were received in the reception-room, and some chairs, intended solely for such occasions, (for neither the King nor the members of his household sit on chairs,) were offered us. After waiting a few minutes, his Majesty, tastefully arrayed in a cloth of plaid velvet, and gold embroidered slippers, presented himself, and was introduced to his visitors respectively. The interview lasted about an hour. I told him briefly, through the interpreter, our object in visiting Africa, which seemed to give him much pleasure: so far as his dominions extended, he said, emigrants might select land suitable to their purpose, and he would gladly give it. I thanked him for his offer, and then spoke for a few minutes of the great results which must flow from the development of a country like his, so blessed with resources. In reference to an American emigrant who came with me from Manchester, he inquired whether he understood using oxen for agricultural purposes: when answered in the affirmative, he seemed rather incredulous. The other gentlemen had also business to transact with the King, which rendered our conversation rather brief.

When I had been a few days at Lagos, Mr. Williams, a somewhat intelligent native, interpreter to the Consul, invited me to see his farm on the mainland, a few miles across the river. Accompanied by two other persons, we left early in the morning before breakfast, expecting to return in two hours at most. Reaching the land, it was still necessary to journey a few miles to the farm: though yet early, it was warm, and the walk tiresome, so that I was obliged to rest myself on a stump while my companions proceeded to a little distance to plant some seed. Seeing a bird which I wanted to preserve, alight a few yards off, I tried to come within shot of it: before able to do so, it pursued its flight. I followed and eventually shot it, but in attempting to return I unfortunately took a direction leading away from my first position. I wandered about for more than two hours, shouting all the time at the top of my voice to attract attention, for my ammunition being in the possession of my companions, I could not fire my gun for that purpose. I soon found myself in the midst of an almost impenetrable jungle, the shrubbery and vines so thickly interlacing, that it was with the greatest difficulty I could break through : the ground too was swampy, and I sometimes sunk nearly to my knees. By this time my friends were as busy seeking me. I never felt more joyful than when I heard their voice in response to my own. From hunger, fatigue, heat of the sun, and excitement, I returned home about 2 P.M., with severe headache and fever. The next day I was worse, and continued ill for several days. The reader has here my first initiation into the African fever, and I might add that not a few may trace their first attack to similar imprudence. In such a climate a stranger should never leave his home before breakfast, nor undertake very vigorous exercise before he has passed the ordeal of acclimature.

CHAPTER III

JOURNEY TO ABBEOKUTA.

The Crowthers—River Ogun—Ogboi Creek—Nymphæa—Rhizophora Mangle—Villages in the Swamp—Steam Navigation on the Ogun—Fish-Snares—Current—Rocky Bed—Crossing on Calabashes—"Agayen"—Subterranean Streams—Aro—Orange Cottage.

I REMAINED at Lagos nearly six weeks, and my colleague, Dr. Delany, not having arrived, I determined on at once setting out for Abbeokuta. I left on the 29th of August, accompanied by Messrs. Samuel and Josiah Crowther, sons of the worthy native missionary, the Rev. Samuel Crowther.

The journey from Lagos to Abbeokuta is usually made by canoes, up the river Ogun, the waters of which empty into the bay of Lagos. Somewhat west of its embouchure is the Ogboi creek or cut, communicating with the Ogun about ten or twelve miles from the bay. Canoe-men always prefer reaching the river by means of this cut, as the distance direct up the river is greater. There was abundance of the beautiful water-plant "Nymphæa," now in flower, in places where the current was gentle. The land on both sides the cut is low, swampy and thickly covered with mangrove, (*Rhizophora Mangle*.) Notwithstanding this, there are two villages in the midst of the swamps, the inhabitants of which enjoy good health, affording an example of a fact often noticed in the West-Indies and tropical America, that people might live with impunity in the midst of regions from which is constantly distilled the most dangerous miasma.*

The Ogun is navigable for steam-vessels of not over five feet draft during seven or eight months of the year, namely, from about a fortnight after the first rainy season in May, to December, about a month after the cessation of the last rains. After this time the quantity of water diminishes rapidly, so that in February and March an infant could easily ford it at places where it was not long before as deep and wide as the Schuylkill at Philadelphia.

Vessels of the same draft can during the other four or five months always ascend as far as Gaun, about one third the distance. There being plenty of water at the time I ascended, the journey to Abbeokuta took five days. When the river is very high, or, as in the last of the dry season, has but little water,

---

* See similar example in Backie's Narrative, p. 195.

the journey takes from ten to fifteen days. In the former case it is necessary to proceed very slowly and cautiously along the margin of the water, where frequent obstructions are encountered, and in the latter, the water being in many places only a few inches deep, the canoes must often be unloaded and sometimes carried over places where they could not possibly float. At any time, however, except in the height of the rainy season when the roads are much flooded, the journey can be performed by land in two or three days. The water is of a whitish tinge, from holding in suspension argilaceous matter and minute fragments of the constituents of granite, particularly feldspar. There is abundance of fish, to catch which the natives attach snares to strong ropes made from the stems of a species of creeping palm, (*Calamus*,) passed across the river and fastened on both sides to trees. These ropes offer some impediments to navigation, frequently upsetting canoes, and causing the loss of their freight. The current, to within ten or fifteen miles of Lagos, is very strong, due doubtless to the regular but very marked elevation of the interior country. There is generally an annual overflow of its banks. Although far more water falls in the former rainy season in May, June and July, than during the latter in September, October and November, yet the river never overflows till in the latter season, since the former rains are eagerly absorbed by the soil, which with every thing else is then exceedingly dry from the prevalence of the harmattan winds immediately previous. Many large trees are then washed away and drifted into the channel, which are very troublesome to travellers on the river. There are extensive forests on the banks, from which fuel could be obtained in abundance, and which would furnish considerable freight in the form of timber to both Abbeokuta and Lagos. It offers also fine facilities in some places for water-power.

Above Abbeokuta, on account of the very rocky character of its bed, the Ogun is not navigable even for canoes. At places, however, where it intersects the roads, canoes could in the rainy season be used with advantage to convey goods and passengers across, but the natives use instead large calabashes, on which the passenger sits, the ferryman swimming and pushing his freight before him. They not only prefer the use of calabashes, but will have nothing whatever to do with canoes, and affect to despise those who use them. Not unfrequently I heard the term "agayen" reproachfully applied by the people of the interior towns to my interpreter and other persons from places on or near the sea-coast. The word simply means canoe-men.

I crossed the Ogun in three places above Abbeokuta;

the first time between Oyo and Isehin, next between Biocu and Beracudu, and finally between the last place and Abbeokuta, distant respectively five days, two days, and two hours' journey from Abbeokuta, the day's journey being from twenty-five to thirty miles. At these places I found the bed of the river covered to such an extent with masses of granite rock, that it could be easily crossed dryshod by stepping from stone to stone, although fully twenty-five yards wide. I found also the water wider and deeper than it is from Abbeokuta to ten miles below. The reason of this perhaps is that the irregular rocky surface of its bed above Abbeokuta retards the progress of the water, and for the same reason it is not absorbed as it is below Abbeokuta, where the bed is sandy. We found all through the country brooks and rivulets apparently dry in some places, while at other points lower down the course, the water was gushing out clear and sweet. It is possible too to procure water by making slight excavations in the apparently dry sandy beds of what had been in the rainy season impassable rivers.

On the 4th September we arrived at Aro, where we found horses awaiting us, for the Crowthers had sent before to order them. Aro is the landing-place for the city of Abbeokuta in the rainy season; Agbamiya, a point lower down the river, being used in the dry season.

It, the former is four miles below Ake, the business centre of the city, and about a mile and a half from the city gate. Above Aro the river is too rocky to permit canoes to ascend into the city. This place is doubtless destined to become of considerable importance; already all the merchants have depots there, and hereafter will also find it of advantage to make it their residence, when it is likely to be included in the city limits. In little more than an hour after we left Aro, we were comfortably domiciled at "Orange Cottage," the beautiful little dwelling of my kind companions, the Crowthers.

CHAPTER IV.

ABBEOKUTA.

Introduction to the "Alake"—Royal attire—Wives, over one hundred—Ogboni Elders—Native Game, *Wari*—Visit to the Chiefs.

ACTING-CONSUL Lieut. Lodder had furnished me with a letter of introduction to his Majesty Okukenu, Alake of Abbeokuta, which I was anxious to present. The Reverend Henry Townsend of the Church Missionary Society kindly accompanied me. My reception by the King was very cordial. I explained to him the object of my visit to the country, which he was pleased to hear. He observed that for people coming with such purposes, and for missionaries, he had great " sympathy," and would afford every encouragement; but that some of the people (emigrants from the Brazils, Cuba, and Sierra Leone) who were now coming into his dominion, especially traders, gave him much trouble. His body above the loins was nude; otherwise his attire consisted of a handsome velvet cap trimmed with gold, a costly necklace of coral, and a double strand of the same ornament about his loins, with a velvet cloth thrown gracefully about the rest of his person, under which he wore his shocoto, a sort of loose trowsers reaching only to the knees. One of his wives (he has more than a hundred) was seated on the same mat fanning him. He fondled on his knees an infant, and eight or ten of his other little children, all about the same age, were gamboling around him. On his right were seated several very old men dressed in white cloths, elders of the Ogboni council, with one or other of whom his majesty usually plays at the native game of *wari*, a description of which is given in another place. He offered me the only chair in his establishment. The Reverend Mr. Townsend, being an intimate acquaintance, sat on an end of his mat. A few slaves, by the by, his chief administrative officers, also sat near him. He presented me on my departure a head of cowries, worth nearly fifty cents. During the next few days I visited the principal chiefs, to explain the object of my visit and to make to each a small present. Though humble, these presents were well received and in every instance a return present of cola nuts, (*cola sterculia acuminata,*) or of cowries was given. The natives generally at first regarded me as a white man, until I informed them of my connection with the Negro. This announcement always gained me a warmer reception.

The reader here will permit me to digress to explain

a matter respecting which there has hitherto been some misconception. It has been asserted that the native African does not manifest under any circumstance the same deference for colored men, as he does for white men; and so fully is this believed, particularly in the United States, that both my colleague Dr. Delany and myself were frequently cautioned respecting the danger to which we should be exposed in consequence of our complexion. It is indeed true that more respect has been accorded to white men, on account of their superior learning and intelligence, than to the generality of semi-civilized black men from the Brazils and other places, who now live in the Aku country; but it is a great mistake to think that the same is withheld from colored men similarly endowed with their white brethren. Let any disinterested person visiting Abbeokuta, place himself in a position to notice the manner in which such a person, for instance, as the Reverend Samuel Crowther, or even his son of the same name, each a pure Negro, is treated, and he would soon perceive the profound respect with which Africans treat those of their own race worthy of it. The white man who supposes himself respected in Africa, merely because he is white, is grievously mistaken. I have had opportunities to know, that if he should, presuming on his complexion, disregard propriety in his bearing towards the authorities, he would receive as severe rebuke as a similar offense would bring him in England. One of the chiefs of Abbeokuta, Atambala, was with us one day when a young missionary entered, and passed him with only a casual nod of the head. As soon as he was seated the haughty old chief arose and said, in his own tongue: "Young man, whenever any of my people, even the aged, approaches me, he prostrates himself with his face to the ground. I do not expect the same from you, or from civilized men, (*oyibo*,) nevertheless remember always that I shall demand all the respect due to a chief of Abbeokuta." A sufficient apology was given, and the matter ended, not without, it is hoped, teaching a salutary lesson.

The king of Abbeokuta, whose person is considered too sacred for the popular gaze, is never permitted to leave the palace except on special occasions, and then he only goes into the open space without the palace-gates, one of his wives being in attendance to screen his face with a large fan. So with the king of Oyo, who once or twice only in the year exhibits himself to the public, decorated in his best robes and wearing a crown of coral. At these times any one can stare at his majesty with impunity. In Ilorin the king may not be seen, except as a mark of special favor, even by those to whom he affords the privilege of an audience.

If the reader will permit the expression, Abbeokuta might be said to be in form an irregular circle. The circumference of its outer wall, for in some parts of the city there are three walls, is about twenty-three miles. It was originally formed of over one hundred townships, each independent and governed by its own chief. The people are of the Egba tribe of the Akus, sometimes incorrectly called Yorubas. About fifty years ago, wars with the surrounding tribes, particularly with the Yorubas, had disorganized their nation, the greatest number of their people being enslaved, and sent to the Brazils, Cuba, and other places; many of them were also recaptured by British cruisers and taken to Sierra Leone. A few flying before their relentless enemy, and wandering from place to place, at length found refuge beneath a shelf of rock now called " Olumo;" this hiding-place is said to have been before the den of a band of robbers. Advantage was taken of the security thus afforded, by others of the Egba tribe, and their number continued to increase until they felt strong enough to form a town and build a wall. In a short time that town, as before stated, contained the remnants of over one hundred townships, and became too powerful to be successfully assaulted by their enemies. The walls now include a number of huge hills of superior building granite, the quarrying of which will doubtless yield large profit to its inhabitants at no remote day.

They called the town very appropriately, "Abbeokuta," which means under a rock. It is now estimated to contain more than one hundred thousand inhabitants, and its population is fast increasing by accessions, not only from the surrounding tribes, who find in it greater security for life and property, but also from many of those, and their descendants, who were sold away as slaves.

Although the people have increased, one is at a loss to divine what has become of the chiefs of so many townships. One after another they have fallen off, and their successors have either never been appointed or are too insignificant to command attention. The treaty we concluded with the authorities of the place was signed by only seven chiefs, the king's signature not included. To them we were sent specially by the king, an act which seemed to indicate, either that they alone were of sufficient consequence to take part in such a matter, or that they, by common consent, were deemed the representatives of the rest.

The language of the Egbas, is the same as that of the Yorubas, Ijebus and other neighboring tribes, concerning which the author of "Polyglotta Africana" makes the following just remarks: "For the last few years they have very erroneously made use of the name Yoruba, in reference to the whole nation, supposing that the Yoruba is the most powerful Aku tribe, but the appellation is liable to far greater objection than that of Aku, and ought to be forthwith abandoned; for it is, in the first place, unhistorical, having never been used of the whole Aku nation by any body, except for the last few years conventionally by the missionaries; secondly, it involves a twofold use of the word 'Yoruba,' which leads to a confusion of notions; for in one instance the same word has to be understood of a whole, in another only of a part; and thirdly, the name being thus incorrect, can never be received by the different tribes as a name for the whole nation."

Viewed as to its power of enforcing order, and affording security for life and property, the government of Abbeokuta is as efficient as a civilized government can be, and it accomplishes these ends with the greatest ease and simplicity. Punishment is always summary and certain; notwithstanding, nobody complains of injustice. The penalty for theft is extreme, being either decapitation or foreign slavery. Before the advent of missionaries and civilized people adultery was sometimes also a capital offense; now it is modified to heavy fines, the amount of which is always proportioned to the position and wealth of the offender. Cases of adultery often occur, and must be expected until they are taught to abandon the disgusting system of polygamy.

The tenure of property is as it is among civilized people, except as to land, which is deemed common property; every individual enjoys the right of taking unoccupied land, *as much as he can use*, wherever and whenever he pleases. It is deemed his property as long as he keeps it in use; after that, it is again common property. This custom is observed by all the Akus.

The surviving relatives of one buried on any lot of ground, have a right to that ground which nothing can tempt them to relinquish, and from respect to the sentiment, no one would invade, on any pretext, particularly when the deceased was a mother or father. Mr. S. Crowther, Jr., has long desired to possess a strip of land contiguous to his place of business, but no offer of money can induce the owner to part with it, although he is very poor; because his father lies buried there.

CHAPTER V

NATIVE AUTHORITIES.

Peculiarity of Government—"Ibashorun" or Prime Minister—Shukenu—"His Highness Ogubonna," Friend of Civilization—"You are of my own kindred"—Atambala—Agé—Mr. Crowther and the Doctors—Order of Succession—Departments of Government—Shodeke.

THE government of Abbeokuta is peculiar, combining the monarchical, the patriarchal, and no small share of the republican. Almost every free man, woman and child is a member of the Ogboni Lodge, of which there is one in every township or chiefdom. These lodges are presided over by elders of their own election, and the elders at the decease of the chief choose his successor from his relatives, generally his brother, seldom or never from among his own sons, as hereafter explained. The successor of the king is also choosen by the chiefs and elders combined, their act being subsequently ratified by the people, assembled *en masse*. It is in this that the republican element of the government of Abbeokuta is recognized. There is, as already observed, a king, the Alake, or chief of Ake, which place ranks first among the numerous townships. He is a good-natured fat old gentleman, giving himself only so much concern about public affairs as to secure the good will of his rather turbulent chiefs, to whom perhaps a ruler of more active temperament would be less welcome; there are times, however, when he has been roused to great energy and decision of character. Next in order of authority is the Ibashorun or Prime Minister, who is also in times of war commander in chief. He too is a man of rather cumbersome proportions, powerful on account of his wealth and the number of soldiers his household furnishes in time of war, still, not personally celebrated for military prowess. The chief next in order is Shukenu, perhaps more corpulent than the Ibashorun. Wealthy, powerful, haughty and courageous, he is nevertheless not free from the charge of cruelty. Scarcely a chief in Africa afforded us a more hearty welcome. Ogubonna, or as the English, to whom he is well known, style him, " His Highness Ogubonna," comes next. He calls himself, not inappropriately, the Friend of Civilization; he is a man of large stature, fine proportion, and in all as fine-looking a Negro as I ever saw. No one could mistake him for any other than a chief, so commanding and dignified is his bearing. On the occasion of my first visit to his Highness, as usual he was informed of my African origin. " From what part of Africa," asked he, "did your grandmother come?" As this was a point on which I possessed no information, I could not give him a satisfactory answer. He remained silent for a short time, and at last said: "How can I tell but that you are of my own kindred, for many of my ancestors were taken and sold away." From that day he called me relative, and of course as every other African had as good a claim to kindredship, I soon found myself generally greeted as such.

Adjoining the American Baptist Mission Station, at which we sojourned while at Abbeokuta, is the compound of the chief Atambala. Less powerful and wealthy than his colleagues, he is still a very important personage in the councils of the nation, chiefly on account of his cunning. Every important mission requiring the exercise of such characteristic, is intrusted to him, and it is seldom that he fails: he is also a great orator. In personal appearance he is tall, but not as stout as the other chiefs spoken of above, and although fully eighty years old, he maintains much youthful vigor and comeliness. I am indebted to him for many kind offices. There are the names of three other chiefs attached to our treaty, but my acquaintance with them arose from only a single interview, and I am therefore unable to speak of them. I might, however, be permitted to mention that at our interview with Agé, whose name is found mentioned last in our treaty, as usual it was necessary to mention my origin, for the Africans are not as keen in the recognition of their descendants, as are the Americans of the same class of persons. On learning this, he took hold of my hand and shook it heartily; and drawing me toward him, he threw his arms about my neck, and pressed me with warmth. He has since died: for many months he was a cripple. No one has been more conspicuous in the affairs of his country, or was more respected by his people, than this good old man.

There are many doctors—physicians, I might have said—throughout the Aku country; and they are as jealous of their profession, and as opposed to innovation in practice, as the most orthodox disciple of Æsculapius amongst us can be. Shortly after the return of Mr. S. Crowther, Jr., from London, where he received the training of a surgeon, several of these doctors, hearing that he was prescribing for many who were before their patients, assembled *en masse* in the market-place, and after due deliberation issued an "injunction" that he should forthwith abandon his practice. Some of the foremost of them were deputed to communicate the decree of the faculty. They were cordially received, and heard with patience. After some conversation, Mr. C. informed them that he was willing to obey, but only after a trial on both sides should prove him to be the less skilled in the mysteries of the profession. To this they consented. Time was given for preparation on both sides. In the afternoon the regulars appeared, clothed in their most costly garments, and well provided with orishas or charms attached to all parts of their persons and dress. In the mean time Mr. Crowther had also prepared to receive them. A table was placed in the middle of the room, and on it a dish in which were a few drops of sulphuric acid, so placed that a slight motion of the table would cause it to flow into a mixture of chlorate of potassa and white sugar. A clock was also in the room, from which a small bird issued every hour, and announced the time by cooing. This was arranged so as to coo while they were present. Mr. Crowther then made a brief harangue, and requested them to say who should lead off in the contest. This privilege they accorded to him. The door was closed, the curtains drawn down. All waited in breathless expectation. Presently the bird came out, and to their astonishment cooed twelve times, and suddenly from the midst of the dish burst forth flame and a terrible explosion. The scene that followed was indescribable: one fellow rushed through the window and scampered; another in his consternation, overturning chairs, tables and every thing in his way, took refuge in the bed-room, under the bed, from which he was with difficulty afterwards removed. It need not be added that they gave no more trouble, and the practice they sought to break up was only the more increased for their pains.

Although the person made king must be of the royal family, yet a son seldom succeeds, but usually a brother by the same mother, or a son of a sister, also of the same mother. Such a person is certainly a relative, while from circumstances growing out of the system of polygamy, the son of from fifty to two hundred wives might not be the child of the husband. Property also descends in the same manner.

The appointment of the king devolves on the chiefs and elders of the Ogboni, the latter of course all old men. Some of them are men of great influence themselves, and as their power would be limited by an efficient monarch, they are not likely to choose such.

The King, or Alake, as he is called, is not, as in civilized countries, the executive: his office seems to be more to preside at all important councils. He exercises other functions not well understood by strangers. The government is divided into several departments. The Elders constitute the judiciary. The officers of the Ogboni,* a secret order, exercise legislative func-

---

* This order is accessible to persons of any age or sex, but not to slaves.

tions. The executive department devolves on Oro, an imaginary deity, of which mention shall be made hereafter.

The present Alake succeeded Shodeke, a man so venerated as to be ranked among the demigods. Every one who knew him has something to recount of the virtue of Shodeke.

The support of the king and chiefs is derived from the offerings of their slaves, and of those who bring controversies to them for settlement.

CHAPTER VI.

MISCELLANEOUS.

African Cities—Forms of "Compounds"— Native Food — Clothing — Industry — Percolator — Blacksmiths — Iron-smelting — Weaving — Farming Implements — Indigo — Palm-oil Factories — "Taffi" — Traders — Personal Habits — Cola-nuts — Native Affability—Onoshoko, "Father of the King"—Polygamy—Slavery—African Honor — Symmetry of Form — Calisthenics—Archery—Native Games of Skill—Stray Fact—Wild Bees—An Adventure—Funeral—Processions—Discovery of Abbeokuta.

In African native cities there are no streets such as would be called so in a civilized country. The houses or compounds are scattered according to the discretion or taste of their owners; lanes, always crooked, and frequently very narrow, being left between them. These dwellings are sometimes very large, including in many instances accommodation for from twenty to two hundred inmates, especially in those of some of the wealthier chiefs, which are sometimes tenanted by over three hundred people.

The usual form of a compound is square, and is bounded by a wall against which the rooms are commonly built. The walls are of mud, but are sometimes very straight and smooth. In some of the mission-houses, which are likewise of mud, but plastered, a stranger would not suspect the material.

In the area within the inclosure are gathered their sheep, goats and so forth, at nights. In almost every one of these dwellings there is a large dove-cot, in which are bred hundreds of common domestic pigeons. They are very fond of raising chickens, ducks and other poultry.

The food of the Egbas, as well as of all the tribes between Lagos and Ilorin, is very simple, consisting chiefly of a preparation called *eko:* corn is macerated in water until fermentation ensues. It is then crushed between stones, and the chaff separated by washing. The milky liquor is then boiled in large pots until it assumes a consistency somewhat stiffer than cream, which as it cools becomes as firm as jelly. The taste is rather unpleasant at first, but one seldom fails to like it after persisting in its use. A portion of it nearly as large as a penny-roll, wrapped in leaves, is sold for five cowries, or about a mill. An adult native consumes from four to eight at a meal, taking with it as a relish a few spoonsful of *obé*, or "palaver-sauce," as the Sierra Leone folks call it. Palaver-sauce is made by cooking together palm-oil, pepper, ocros,* locust-seed,

---

* Abelmoschus (Hibiscus) Esculentus.

ogiri and several esculent herbs. Leaving out the ogiri, which stinks dreadfully, *obé* is certainly very fine, but the natives greatly prefer it with ogiri, just as certain Epicureans do tainted venison. Ground beans and pepper, fried in oil, called *acras;* cooked yams, beaten with water in a wooden mortar, *fufu;* with certain other preparations of corn, rice, etc., also form part of their diet. Native beer or *oti* is plentiful, cheap and sometimes good. It is made either from maize or Guinea corn. As with the brewing of beer in civilized countries, the grain is suffered to germinate in order to develop saccharine matter. They have, however, no means of arresting fermentation, and hence the beer can not keep. Another very fine drink is made from the sap which flows from incisions made in the palm-tree.

The people are not nude, as many suppose Africans to be generally. Of course we except children, and even they are not always so. The apparel of a man consists of a shocoto, cloth and cap. The shocoto is a sort of loose trowsers, fastened with a string directly above the hips. He dispenses with the cloth when at labor. Instead of this cloth the wealthy wear a tobe, a loose large garment, worn over the shoulders, and falling below the knees: they are generally handsomely embroidered. Sometimes, however, a cloth of velvet, silk or some other expensive material is substituted. Instead of the shocoto, men and boys are sometimes seen with garments made exactly like the kilts of the Scotch Highlanders; the cloth too is worn in much the same way as the Highlander's plaid. The attire of the women is even more simple, consisting of one or two cloths passed round the body. They wear besides a sort of turban, and in a few instances, another cloth over the breast and shoulders. The costume of some Africans costs as much as that of many of the most extravagant dandies of civilized countries.

We met several of those individuals who though entirely of Negro parentage, are white, from the absence of pigmentum or coloring matter from the skin, hair and eyes; both in features and texture of hair, however, they still resemble the Negro. But little is known of this phenomenon, notwithstanding the fact that it is common to all races of men, and even to inferior animals, white horses, birds, mice, etc., being often seen. A fact which we observed, is perhaps not yet known, namely, that between the albino proper, and those in whom there is a normal development of pigmentum, there are individuals possessing more or less color, so that if a series were formed embracing both extremes, the difference between any consecutive two would be hardly perceptible. The first digressions are characterized by a reddish tinge of hair, and complexion in harmony, but difficult to describe. These characteristics are observed still more prominent in other individuals, and thus on, till some are found with complexions as light as mulattoes, although not otherwise like them. From these the deviation still continues, till at length the perfect albino is found. Albinos, whether of the Indian, Negro or white race, are not uncommon in America, but they seldom attract attention, as without particular observation they seem like ordinary white men. For instance, one of the most prominent editors of a daily newspaper in New-York, is an albino. The term was first applied by the Portuguese towards these people. They can not well endure exposure to bright daylight, their eyes lacking the protection which is afforded to others by the color in the iris, etc.

Not long since, and even now, there are not a few who regard the African to be like the snake or alligator, a lazy creature, whose life is spent basking in the sunshine, and subsisting on roots and herbs or whatever else of food within reach of his arm. A Negro friend of mine mentioned to no less a personage than a professor in a medical school in America, that he had read in the work of Denham and Clapperton, that women are commonly seen in Africa spinning by the road-side, and selling boiled potatoes, roast-meats, etc. "Nonsense," said he, "that is all English romance: can you believe such folly?" Nevertheless I assert, and appeal to every one who has visited this section of Africa to verify my assertion, that there is not a more industrious people on the face of the earth. Rise as early as you please and enter a native compound, and you will there find the women engaged at their varied occupations. Go at night as late as you please, and there by the feeble light of her lamp she is seen in the act of labor, spinning, weaving or preparing food for the ensuing day. There is not a child among the Akus—I say nothing of other African tribes—who is not instructed in some means of realizing a living. The men are builders, blacksmiths, iron-smelters, tanners and leather-workers, tailors, carpenters, calabash-carvers, weavers, basket, hat and mat-makers, farmers: the women weave, spin, dye, cook, brew, make pots, oils, soap and I know not what else.

Not many years since, much attention was excited among practical chemists by the invention of the Percolator, an apparatus for extracting in a very short time the virtues of medicinal herbs, etc. Essentially the same contrivance is used, and has been used from time immemorial by the native Africans, in making lye from ashes for the manufacture of soap, and for dyeing. A small aperture is made in the bottom of a large earthen vessel, which is covered with straw and then filled with ashes. This is placed over a similar vessel, so as slightly to enter it. Water is then suffered to percolate slowly through the first vessel into the second, which as it does so extracts all the soluble matter from the ashes.

Although the native blacksmiths frequently execute very fine productions of their art, yet their apparatus is very rude. They work sitting on the ground. Their bellows is hewn out of a block of wood about three feet long, and six or seven inches deep, in the form of two cups connected by a tube, to the middle of which another tube of clay is attached, through which the current of air is propelled. The two cavities are each covered with a sack of untanned hide, and a stick of wood about three feet long is fastened to each sack. A little boy having hold of the ends of these sticks, lifts and depresses them alternately, and thus secures the action. Although different in appearance, these bellows operate on the same principle as those of civilized construction. For fuel they use charcoal made from the hard shell surrounding the kernel of the palm-nut.

I passed through two iron-smelting villages on the road between Oyo and Isehin in Yoruba, but they were not in operation, as the war, of which mention shall be made hereafter, had driven the inhabitants into the larger towns for protection. The furnaces, or the portion of them above the surface of the earth, are made of clay. They are in the form of cylinders, about thirty inches high; the diameter of the bases about six feet. A hole is made in the upper base, communicating both with six or seven similar holes around the convex surface, and, by a small orifice, with a large cavity underground and beneath the cylinder. In this, immediately under the orifice, I found a mass of slag. They use charcoal for fuel, which they produce in abundance in the forests in the midst of which these villages are usually located.

The apparatus of the weavers is very simple. There are two kinds, one used by the men, producing cloth of only a few inches in width, and another by the women, producing cloth as wide as of English manufacture. The men can make cloth of an indefinite length: the apparatus used by the women limits the length of the cloth to about two and a half yards. I forbear a description of either of these contrivances, as such as I could make would hardly be intelligible.

The implements of the farmers are only two, a billhook and hoe. The hoe is not bad in itself, but very badly mounted for use by a civilized farmer. The handles are short, rendering it necessary for the operator to stoop in using them. The soil is prepared by heaping the surface-earth in hills, close together and regularly in parallel lines. Cotton, yams, corn, cassava, beans, grow close together in the same field.

The beautiful blue, almost purple dye of their cloths is not from the common indigo-plant of the East and West-Indies, but from a large climbing plant. The leaves and shoots are gathered while young and tender. They are then crushed in wooden mortars, and the pulp made up in balls and dried. For dyeing, a few of these balls are placed in a strong lye made from ashes, and suffered to remain until the water becomes offensive from the decomposition of vegetable matter. The cloths are then put in, and moved about until sufficiently colored. There are dyeing establishments in all the towns from Lagos to Ilorin.

Palm-oil factories, as one would suppose from the quantity of the oil exported from Lagos and other parts of the West-African coast, are very numerous. The process of extracting the oil is simple. The nuts are gathered by men. From one to four or five women separate them from the integuments. They are then passed on to other women, who boil them in large earthen pots. Another set crush off the fibre in mortars. This done, they are placed in large clay vats filled with water, and two or three women tread out the semi-liquid oil, which comes to the surface as disengaged from the fiber, where it is collected and again boiled to get rid of the water which mechanically adheres to it. The inner surface of these clay vats, having at first absorbed a small quantity of oil, is not afterwards affected either by the water or oil. It is said that palm-oil loses its color by being kept for some time at the boiling temperature.

No part of the palm-nut is wasted. The oil being extracted, the fibre, which still retains some oil, is dried and used for kindling. The kernel is used for making another oil, *adi*, excellent for burning in lamps and making native soap. The hard shell or pericarp is burnt for charcoal and used by the native blacksmiths. They prepare several other kinds of oil, such as agusi, beni, and ori, or shea butter. The last, which possesses medicinal virtues, is now exported from Abbeokuta.

Palm-oil, considering the profit which it brings the manufacturer, the abundant growth of the plant which yields it, and the great and increasing demand for it, is destined to become of great commercial importance.

The native women all through the country prepare from the juice of the sugar-cane, by boiling, a sort of "taffi." The cane is cut in short bits, crushed in a large wooden mortar, and the juice wrung out, filtered and boiled to the consistence of candy. While at Ilorin and without sugar, we often used this preparation to sweeten our coffee. The reader who knows any thing of the process of sugar-making will perceive from this that all the knowledge necessary to make these people sugar-makers, is that a small quantity of lime must be added to the juice in order to correct the acidity which begins to generate as soon as it is expressed. In this way many of the peasantry of the West Indies prepare their own sugar, and often also for sale.

The Akus are great traders. Such a thing as overreaching them in a bargain is unknown. In no instance do they ever charge for an article what they expect to get for it. "How much for this?" says the purchaser. "One head," replies the vender. "Won't you take forty strings?" "Bring on your cowries," is the reply. "Won't you take thirty strings?" "Bring on your money:" and thus on until the minimum is attained, when he replies: "Not a cowrie less." If the price suits the purchaser, well; if not, he passes on to another trader, when much the same dialogue ensues.

Several of the personal habits of the natives are remarkable. The men universally shave, not only the beard, but the eye-brows, within the nostrils, (the native razors are adapted to this,) and frequently the entire head. Many leave a strip of hair from the forehead, over the crown of the head, down to the back of the neck. The Mohammedans leave also a little tuft of hair on the chin. We met two or three men at Ilorin with whiskers. The margin of the eye-lids is blackened with pulverized sulphuret of antimony, which every native carries about with him for the purpose. The women dye the palm of the hands, finger-nails and feet with ground camwood. Sometimes when about to participate in religious observances, their entire person is colored in this way. They pay great attention to the teeth, using the chewed ends of certain roots for the purpose of brushes, as do the people of the West-Indies, where the custom was doubtless introduced by Africans. Except some little children, we met nobody who did not use tobacco. It is used in the form of snuff, not taken into the nostrils, but on the tongue. A small quantity of benin-seed and of *lubi*, a native impure carbonate of soda, is ground with the snuff. They use the Brazilian roll-tobacco, about twenty per cent of the weight of which is treacle. There are a few who smoke, principally emigrants from Sierra Leone, Cuba and the Brazils.

As might be expected, the use of ardent spirits is very common; yet the natives are seldom seen drunk, the regulations of their Ogboni lodges forbidding it.

Cola-nuts, (*cola acuminata,*) a bitter and slightly astringent vegetable, are used by all, although in some places expensive. It probably counteracts the effects of the laxative character of their food. Whenever any one wishes to show particular mark of respect to his guest, he presents him, with great formality, a few cola-nuts. A little boy or girl brings a covered vessel, the best in the house, and prostrating, presents it. Abundant thanks and salutations follow. They have a proverb which says: " Anger draws arrows from the quiver: good words draw cola-nuts from the bag."*

There is not a more affable people found any where than are the Akus. Not even Frenchmen are more scrupulous in their attention to politeness than they. Two persons, even utter strangers, hardly ever pass each other without exchanging salutations, and the greatest attention is paid to the relative social position of each in their salutations. Equals meeting will simply say, *acu;* but one addressing a superior affixes some word to *acu,* thus, *acabo,* (*acu abo,* †) *acuni,* etc

---

* See Crowther's Vocabulary of the Yoruba language.
† One vowel dropped for euphony.

The superior usually salutes first, and when the disparity of position is great, the inferior prostrates. The young always prostrate to the aged. Women kneel, but never prostrate. Sons, without reference to age or rank, prostrate to their mothers or senior female relatives. They never suffer any thing to interfere with the observance of these courtesies. There is an appropriate salutation for every occasion for instance: *acuaro*, good morning; *acuale*, good evening; *acushe*, for being industrious; *acabo*, or *acuabo*, (*ua* as diphthong,) for returning from a journey; *acatijo*, for long absence; *acujoco*, for sitting or resting; *acudaro*, for standing or walking; *acuraju*, expressive of sympathy, in distress or sickness; *acueru*, for bearing a burthen; *acualejo*, for entertaining a stranger. So rich is the language in salutations, that the above list could have been increased indefinitely.

At Oyo, the capital of the Yoruba nation, there is an old man, apparently in a very humble position, for no one is more condescending and courteous than he. He is, nevertheless, no less a personage than the Onoshoko, or "Father of the King," an officer of state so called. In the event of the king's demise, the privilege of choosing a successor devolves on him; hence his position is really very exalted: besides, he is the party with whom the king is bound to advise on all important affairs. It is customary for men in high positions, the king's relatives, chief Balaguns, and so forth, to construct in front of their houses certain turret-like contrivances, called by them *akabi*. The king offered Onoshoko to construct akabis in front of his house, as his position and rank demanded them. "No," said the old man, "Onoshoko is well enough without akabis. Let not any one be able to say, from my example, that he too must have akabis: honor belongs to the king only." He is the only man in the kingdom who is privileged to approach the king without prostrating, nevertheless he insists on doing so, explaining his conduct always by the remark that he, in his respect to the king, would ever be an example for others to copy. The king himself, determining not to be outdone, whenever Onoshoko enters the palace-yard, prostrates to the old man; and it is common for those about the palace to see one of them stealthily approaching the other, in order first to assume this position of respect.

Except with the few Africans who have been brought under the influence of Christianity, polygamy is universal. A man's position in society is estimated either by his bravery in war, or his wealth; and he can only manifest the latter by the number of his wives, children and slaves. From this circumstance men are frequently reported wealthy, and yet in emergencies can not raise ten bags of cowries, (about $40.) Wives are commonly engaged at an early age, frequently before six or seven years old. This is done by paying to the parents a stipulated sum, and occasionally making presents both to them and the betrothed. When the engagement is concluded, a bracelet is placed about the wrist to signify the new relation she sustains. She remains with the parents until of proper age to be taken home to her husband. If she comes with honor, two or three days after, adorned with costly cloths and jewels, and with music, she marches with a large company of maidens through the city, to receive the congratulations and presents of her friends, which are generally on such an occasion very liberally bestowed. Otherwise, the parents are made to refund the whole amount advanced in engaging her, and the guilty partner to her infidelity, if known, is prosecuted for adultery. If the intended husband is a youth, never before married, his mother, or less frequently his father, makes the engagement for him; and the parties are respectively kept in ignorance of each other until they are both of suitable age to live together.

A less troublesome way of procuring a wife, with

many, is to resort to the slave-marts of Ilorin at once, money in hand, and make their choice. The latter, of course, are slaves, as well as their children, between whom, however, and other slaves, there is some distinction. Wives procured according to the first of these methods, although not regarded as slaves, are practically as much so as the others, for like them, at the death of their lord they become nominally, and often really, the wives of his eldest son, except, of course, his own mother. They have, however, the privilege of choosing the next elder son, or of observing ever after a state of celibacy, which but few women would choose, as it is regarded reproachfully.

According to their means of procuring them, men possess from a single wife to two or three hundred. Except the chiefs there are few, however, who have more than about twenty. The Yoruba king at Oyo, Adelu, who is reputed the wealthiest man of the Akus, maintains about three hundred wives.* They are never suffered to leave the palace-yard, except on certain days, when they march in procession through the town in charge of eunuchs, of whom the king has

---

* Including the surviving wives of his father, who as already mentioned, are all nominally his, he is said to have about one thousand.

a large number. Men are not suffered to approach them in these excursions. The King of Ilorin and other great personages of his court also keep their wives always confined. In this case, however, they are supported. In Abbeokuta, where even the wives of the king must support themselves, they are permitted to go abroad, and are generally among the most industrious traders of the place.

Inquiry is sometimes made as to whether wives agree among themselves. I answer, they do, as well as a number of women living in the same house can under other circumstances: at any rate, their disputes do not arise from the fact that they are all the wives of the same husband. There is always one, only one, who is intrusted with the domestic affairs of her lord, and to her all the others pay the greatest deference, and they expect the recently married to receive more favor than others: making this philosophic calculation, they are saved much of what, under a different and purer system of morals, would be highly irritating and disgusting.

After polygamy it may be appropriate to make a few remarks respecting its sister evil, slavery, which exists all through this section of Africa. Although the term "slavery" is the only word by which the institution can be properly designated, it is certainly not of the same character as the American institution, there being but little disparity between the condition of the master and that of his slave, since the one possesses almost every advantage accessible to the other. Slaves are often found filling the most exalted positions: thus at Abbeokuta all the king's chief officers are his slaves, and they are among his most confidential advisers. On certain state occasions, one or other of these slaves is often permitted to assume in public the position of the king, and command and receive in his own person the homage and respect due to his master. So in Ilorin, Dungari, the prime minister of the king, daily sits in the market-place to receive the homage of the populace intended for the king, and yet Dungari, really the most important personage of the kingdom, and in rank even above the king's own sons, is a slave. Instances of this kind might be afforded almost indefinitely.

Slaves are procured chiefly by conquest, sometimes in warfare as justifiable and even more so than the wars waged among civilized nations; at other times predatory, and undertaken solely for their capture. Not a few incur slavery as a penalty for crime. Some are sold to defray either their own debts, or it may be the debts of others for which they have become liable; and frequently children are kidnapped and sold away into distant parts.

Although but a few years since every heathen town in this region abounded with slave-markets, there is now, doubtless through the influence of Christian civilization, nothing of the kind seen; and although it would be unsafe to say that slaves are not sometimes sold, yet if so, it is done secretly. The first and only marts we met for "this description of property," were at Ilorin, a Mohammedan kingdom. There was there, besides several small numbers exposed in different places throughout the town, a large market, the Gambari, almost exclusively devoted to their sale, and in which there were certainly not less than from five to six hundred. Christian America and Mohammedan Ilorin do with complacency what the heathens of Yoruba and Egba feel it a disgrace to practise.

At Ilorin we sojourned with Nasamo, the king's sheriff, in whose company only we were permitted to walk about the city. On arriving at the Gambari market in one of our excursions, he pointed to the slaves and jocularly asked whether I wished to purchase. I embraced the opportunity to show him the wrong of making slaves of our fellows, and the great injury which it inflicted not only upon those who suffer, but also on those who practise it. Nasamo fills a high position in the state, and is the master of a large number of slaves; nevertheless he is himself a slave, and doubtless thought of his youthful home and dear parents from whom he was stolen. He admitted all I said, and observed that he wished there was no such thing; but while it existed it was better that they be exposed in the markets than that they should be sold privately, "for then bad men would seize the defenseless and our children, and we would not know where to find them."

The Mohammedans do not sell their co-religionists into slavery: they sometimes hold them as slaves, but only when they were bought as heathens and converted after coming into their possession; but these are never after sold. Here is a vast difference from that class of Christians, so called, who buy and sell the members of their own church, the partakers of the same communion with themselves. How much better are such than the heathens, or even these benighted Mussulmans?

Although, as I have before shown, slavery in Africa is not like slavery in America, or even as it is in Cuba, yet it is still a fact which must not be disregarded, that, more or less, it is slavery—such, it is true, as the teachings and example of good men might quietly but certainly in time overthrow, but which might also by an obverse course assume most of the abhorrent phases of the American institution. My own opposition to slavery does not arise simply from the suffering and ill-treatment which the bondman endures, for in that case I would have to acquit perhaps the majority of American masters. I oppose it because a human being is by it reduced to the condition of a thing, a mere chattel, to be bought or sold at the option of his fellow-man, whose only right to do so is the accidental circumstance of superior power—a power which the good should use to protect rather than oppress the weak. I oppose it because I feel the common instinct that man has an inalienable right to "life, liberty and the pursuit of happiness." Hence I do not regard a slave-owner, even when he makes his slave as comfortable and happy as a slave can be—in all other respects, it may be, as well off as himself—I do not, I say, regard such a person as therefore less guilty: indeed, if there is one class of them whom I detest more heartily than another, it is that class whose course is to render the slave, if possible, contented with his condition.

From this view, therefore, I place my opposition to African slavery on the same ground as to American slavery, and God helping me, shall labor as earnestly for the overthrow of one as for the other.*

* The following distinctions or grades of servitude prevail: one absolutely free through all generations is termed, " *Omo olu wabi.*"

Rev. Mr. Townsend has a small fund at his disposal for assisting slaves to redeem themselves. He has helped by this means several to obtain liberty. The money is usually paid for them without any other condition than a promise to repay it when able to do so. I was told of one instance where a party so helped had not been heard of for two or three years: when he was almost forgotten, he one day appeared and refunded gratefully the whole amount, pleading bad health for not doing so before.

One of the most marked characteristics of the Africans, not only in this section, but all along the Western coast, is the grace and symmetry of their forms, so well yet so unostentatiously displayed by their ordinary costume. Nor can there be any wonder on this account, considering their freedom from all those habits of civilized life so contrary to nature, and which tend so much to the physical deformity that so often offends good taste.

The issue of the child of slave parents, marrying an "*Omo olu wabi,*" is deemed "*eru idili,*" or a slave connected with the family. An absolute slave is called "*eru.*" One in pawn, placed in that condition by another, is termed "*wafa:*" one voluntarily placing himself in pawn is "*Faru so fa.*" A favorite slave, "*eru,*" at the death of his master is seldom if ever considered any longer an *eru,* but becomes "*eru idili,*" and generally marries in the family, in which case his children, if by free mothers, become absolutely free.

One never passes a group of boys at play without witnessing some of the most dexterous performances of tumbling, wrestling and other exercises tending to the development of the muscular powers of the system. In their dances too they exhibit evolutions, throwing at once every muscle into action, which would almost be regarded as impossible except witnessed.

In the towns further interior than Abbeokuta, in which the use of fire-arms has not yet become general, one frequently sees groups of boys contesting in feats of archery, with great skill. In Oyo bets are only permitted in these exercises. There are several fine games of skill practised by the Akus. A favorite one is the "wari." The apparatus consists of twelve cups arranged in two rows, hewn out of a single block of wood. Four bean-like seeds are placed in each cup, and the game is begun by each party alternately taking the contents of one cup of the row next himself and distributing them, one by one, beginning at the cup next to that from which he took them. When one party can throw the last three or four of his beans into the cups of his antagonist, containing not more than one or two beans each, he seizes the contents as his prize, and thus they continue until the beans are all taken, when each counts what he possesses, the victory being of course accorded to him who has most. There is perhaps not a house in which one or more of these apparatus is not kept, for the entertainment of the inmates. They are found too, at all the "beer-shops," if the reader will permit the application of that term to the places at which the native *oti*, or corn-beer, is sold. I never made a more acceptable present to any one, than of four dozen pretty glass balls, or glass marbles, if you please, to the Alake of Abbeokuta, to use in his game of wari. Another game, in which they are frequently seen engaging with much interest, is the *dili*, a kind of tee-ta-too, more complicated, however, and certainly more interesting than that memorable game of our school days. A large square, divided into thirty-six smaller squares, is traced on the ground, on the opposite sides of which the contestants sit. Each is prepared with twelve "men" differently colored. The parties put down one piece alternately, until all are disposed of, when the game is continued by each moving his men from place to place, until he can arrange three of his own on successive squares on a line, which feat entitles him to one of his adversary's men. The effort of each then is, first to procure this arrangement of his own, and next to prevent his adversary from doing likewise. Of course the party capturing most men wins the game.

I insert here a stray fact, lest it should be forgotten. In Abbeokuta and throughout the Aku country, old women are seen *nursing* infants, *not their own*, as in many instances they were far beyond the period of life when such a thing is at all possible.

Wild bees are very common in Africa. One day a large swarm alighted near our house. I essayed to take them in a box, and after two or three unsuccessful attempts, abandoned the undertaking, as it seemed utterly impossible to induce them to take up with a civilized abode. Next morning passing near the box, which was thrown carelessly under a tree, I was surprised to find, that they had quite changed mind, and were busily laboring in their new domicile. They continued several weeks, when ceasing to hear their busy hum, I examined, and found that they had again departed. They carried off, of course, all the honey, but left plenty of wax, which I prepared and brought with me as a sample of African beeswax. The natives thought me a charmed man, because, forsooth, I was not stung to death in the undertaking.

This section of Africa is sometimes the theatre of terrible thunder-storms. In one of these, my colleague, Dr. Delany, accompanied by Reverend Mr. Reed, missionary at Oyo, was caught one night returning from a visit to a friend, some distance from our dwelling.

The doctor rode a young horse, unaccustomed to the road; Mr. Reed's could find its way back on any road it had travelled. The rain fell in torrents, and it was dismally, totally, absolutely dark; being out myself that night, I could not see my own hands, and sometimes, waiting for the flashes of lightning to show the path, my servant would stumble over me, unable to discover any object before him. Every one knows the impossibility of keeping, blindfolded, in a given direction, so we continually deviated from the narrow path, and were in imminent danger of falling into one or other of the numerous excavations from which the natives procure clay to construct their walls. A large rock intercepted the path my friends took returning home, over which Mr. Reed's horse, after some urging, passed, but the Doctor's obstinately refused to follow, and Mr. Reed's as obstinately refused to return. At last they concluded to pass round a little to the right of where they stood to rejoin each other, in trying to effect which both lost their way. Mr. Reed got home with but little trouble, but the Doctor spent half the night wandering over the least inhabited portions of the city, wet to the skin, the rain all the time pouring. He had been but a few days at Abbeokuta, and of course knew nothing of the language. Coming to a native compound, he essayed to attract attention by the use of the two or three words, the pronunciation (not the meaning) of which he knew indifferently. With a loud voice, (the Doctor is a second Stentor,) he cried *acushe!* (a term of salutation to the industrious.) The natives were astonished, and instantly extinguishing their lights, they fled to the recesses of their dwelling, and, although the Doctor exhausted his whole vocabulary in the effort, he could not induce them to stir. After one or two more fruitless attempts at other houses, he at last brought to his aid a few resolute men, who perceiving that he had lost his way, conducted him safe to the dwelling of Mr. Samuel Crowther, Jr., whither I arrived at the same time after a long search to find him.

A funeral in this section of Africa is not unworthy of notice. A brother of the chief Atambala having died during my sojourn at Abbeokuta, I went over to his house to condole with him on his loss. I found the old chief in no condition to receive the sort of condolence I was prepared to offer, as both himself and almost every other person present was intoxicated. His compound* was crowded, a large number of his friends being there to participate in the ceremonies.

---

* Walled inclosures in Africa, comprising several dwellings, are called by the civilized people "compounds."

Drums were beating, the women singing, and as many as had sufficient command of their legs were dancing. They permitted me to see the corpse, and to my astonishment I found it wrapped with cloths, in exactly the same manner as are Egyptian mummies. The cloth is usually the best the friends of the deceased can purchase. On this occasion they used one which I had presented the chief a few days before. It was laid in an open piazza, the walls around which were draped with velvet and other costly cloths. All this time there was moving through the city a procession, made up of drummers, men bearing a board covered with cloths to represent the corpse, women singing alternately songs of lamentation and of praises to the dead, with other men firing guns, and all dancing and otherwise enacting the most extravagant gestures.

The deceased is always buried in the house in which he lived. Sometimes a stone is placed on the spot, on which offerings to his manes are occasionally deposited. In some cases, where the party was greatly respected, on account of his position on earth, he becomes after death the subject of religious adoration.

The Africans are not behind either the English or Americans in their love of pageantry. The writer does not remember a day spent at Abbeokuta without having witnessed something of this sort. The most frequent were processions of societies for mutual saving. They are formed chiefly of women. Once a week each member deposits a certain amount, the aggregate of which is drawn by one member, who of course continues her deposits, and does not draw again, until all in turn have done likewise. There is no disadvantage in drawing last, as those who do so, receive a consideration for the use of their weekly deposits by the other members.

Before 1839 little if any thing was known of Abbeokuta. The Yorubas and Egbas recaptured and taken to Sierra Leone were sold away before any such place existed, and no travellers had before been in the neighborhood, but at this time, vague rumors began to spread along the coast that the different tribes of the Egbas had united themselves, and had built a new city, powerful from its natural defenses not less than for the brave hearts and strong arms of its people. These were joyful tidings indeed to the Egbas at Sierra Leone, in the bosom of most of whom was immediately kindled the strongest desire, again to be united to their long-lost relatives and friends. Conquering a thousand difficulties, they eventually carried out the object of their desire, and in the short time between 1839 and 1842 we are told by Miss Tucker* in her admirable

* "Abbeokuta, or Sunrise within the Tropics." Although Miss

little book that no less than 500 of them left Sierra Leone for their country.

Simultaneously with these occurrences, the people of the Brazils and of Cuba, Egbas, Yorubas, and other Aku tribes who had obtained freedom, began to return. From all sources there are now scattered throughout the country, but chiefly at Lagos and Abbeokuta, over five thousand of these people, semi-civilized generally, but in some instances highly cultivated, being engaged as teachers, catechists, clergymen, and merchants. Industrious, enterprising, and carrying with them, one here and another there, a knowledge of some of the useful arts, they have doubtless been the means of inaugurating a mighty work, which, now that it has accomplished its utmost, must be continued in a higher form by the more civilized of the same race, who for a thousand reasons, are best adapted to its successful prosecution.

The hand of God is in the work, and although many discouragements and impediments might intercept the path of you who would labor for such an end, there is nothing to fear. Persevere, persevere, and the Power, which has already been a safeguard through so many dangers will aid your efforts to the end.

Tucker has never been to Africa herself, yet her statements are perfectly reliable, as they come from the best sources.

CHAPTER VII.

RELIGION

Shango exorcised—Existence of Spirits—Ifa—Agugu—Oro—Aspect of a City on Oro-day—Gymnastic Sports—Pugilistic Encounters—Missions.

THERE are many Mussulmans among the Akus, but chiefly the people are heathens. They acknowledge one supreme being, of whose attributes they have as clear a conception as civilized people generally, but they do not worship him directly, but through subordinate deities representing those attributes. Thus in Shango, the god of thunder, lightning and fire, and the most revered of their deities, the Omnipotence of God is worshipped. Oro represents the retributive power, and Ifa the Omniscience of God. They profess to be sometimes possessed by these deities. The Reverend Mr. Stone, of the American Southern Baptist Mission at Ijaye, once exorcised Shango in a very summary manner from a mischievous boy living in the neighborhood of his dwelling, who, in retaliation for some affront of his parents, had procured a fagot with which he attempted to fire their dwelling. Had he succeeded, a great conflagration might have ensued, from the combustible nature of the materials of the houses. The inmates of the jeopardized dwelling made no other attempt to arrest him in his projects, than pitifully imploring the deity to leave him. Mr. Stone, however, hearing of the affair, procured a rod, and seizing the young scamp soon dispossessed Shango, and so well too, that the god is never likely to possess him again.

They believe in the spirit after death, and in its power of being present among the living for good or evil purposes, hence they frequently resort to the graves of the deceased with offerings, consulting them in affairs of importance, and imploring their protection from the dangers of life.

Ifa, one of their inferior deities, is much resorted to as an oracle. He has a numerous corps of priests, who realize great profit from the offerings made the god, to induce favorable responses. He is consulted by means of a sort of checkerboard, covered with wood-dust, on which the priest traces small squares. The party consulting the god hands him sixteen consecrated palm-nuts, which all the votaries of Ifa carry constantly. He throws them into a small urn, from which taking a few, the number being left to accident, he disposes them at random on the board, and from the order they assume, determines first whether the offering shall be a goat, a sheep, or otherwise; next he ascertains whether the god is satisfied with the offering; if not, he manipulates further to ascertain whether a pair of pigeons or fowls should not be added. The preliminaries being thus arranged, he enters into his business, all the time holding a free and easy conversation with the applicant, through which he is sure to ascertain the kind of responses most welcome.

The *Agugu*, a fantastically attired individual, is frequently seen at Abbeokuta and other places interior. He represents the spirits of the departed, who are frequently consulted through him. No one is permitted to say he is a man, nor to touch him, under penalty of death. If he touches any one, the party touched must die—a dangerous power, it seems, to place in the hands of ignorant men, nevertheless, one never hears of its abuse. He is so dressed as to leave no part of his body exposed, and speaks in a guttural voice, assumed as a disguise.

Next to Shango, *Oro*, as wielding the executive functions of the government, is certainly the most terrible of their subordinate deities. Whenever a malefactor is to be punished, he is given to Oro, and after that no one knows his fate until his head is seen nailed to a tree in an open place before the king's palace. Every night, after the women are within doors, what is called the voice of Oro is heard around the city. It is on this account that the women of Abbeokuta are not permitted to be abroad after dark. The penalty is death to any woman for saying that she knows how the voice is produced, although it is certain that all know. Any man would also be slain for revealing it. This voice is a peculiar whirling noise, produced by a simple mechanism which the reader must conceive for himself, as a description might involve the writer in trouble on his return to Africa. The town is sometimes given to Oro, generally when any important matter is to be considered. This occurred twice during my sojourn there. The day preceding, announcement is made by the town-crier, who goes around ringing, or rather striking a substitute for a bell. On the first occasion I went out early in the morning, determined not to lose, if possible, any part of the ceremonies of the day. The city, usually from the earliest dawn as busy as a hive, was apparently deserted. It was like a body from which animation had fled; and this, all this because woman was not there, her voice was unheard, and her cheerful smile beaming from her countenance on the stranger, even as she toils beneath her heavy yoke, was not seen. A few men and boys were occasionally met, all looking as if discovered in the perpetration of some guilty action, because, forsooth, they were compelled to perform some office regarded, according to their customs, as proper only for women. All the gates of the compounds were carefully closed and watched. I sought and procured admission to two or three of them, and found the women engaged as usual in their varied occupations, except of course, in those which the circumstance compelled men to perform. I continued my perambulations without meeting any thing remarkable until about ten o'clock A.M., when a large number of persons gathered on the open ground in front of the king's palace, singing very prettily and keeping time by striking together two small pieces of very hard wood, which each carried. In a few minutes the king's messenger or lieutenant, with his suite, came out, representing the king. He thanked the company for their praises to the king which formed the burthen of their songs, and having for a few minutes joined with them in a dance, he presented them some cowries and retired. Later in the day I repaired to another part of the city, where I learned several of the elders and chiefs were to meet. Much of the ground was already occupied by young men and boys in active competition for the applause of the crowd which was always liberally accorded to those who performed satisfactorily with their Oro apparatus. Here and there also were other groups, engaged in tumbling, and other active gymnastic sports, which they accomplished excellently. A procession was formed by the elders of the Ogboni lodges and the king's people, and with drums, etc., beginning with the king they went from chief to chief. Of course they remained without the gate. The chief comes out and all together enjoy a vigorous dance. They then sit down, all but one, who praises the chief to his face. A few strings of cowries are then distributed and the procession moves on. Returning homewards late in the afternoon I met some terrible fights. In one instance particularly, a young fellow was most unmercifully whipped. His offense seems to have been of the sort in which one of the other sex was participant. Punishment for these offenses is often reserved for such days when, as on election-days with us, there is greater freedom to engage in pugilistic encounters with impunity.

The next Oro day was only a week before my final departure from Abbeokuta. It was on the occasion of holding a council to consider the duty of the Egbas in relation to a war between the people of Ijaye, their friends and allies, on the one side, and Oyo, and Ibadan on the other. Early in the morning the chiefs and great men of the town, in great state and with many followers, began to assemble in front of the king's palace, at which the king, surrounded by the male members of his household, was seated. There was present the largest concourse of persons I ever witnessed. The young men and boys were engaged as on the other occasion. When all who were to participate in the council had arrived, the king and chiefs repaired to an Ogboni Lodge near, where their business was transacted in secret. This concluded, they returned to the square, to inform the people on what they had determined, and to procure their concurrence, which at Abbeokuta is very essential, particularly as the rulers have no power to execute their designs without the popular arm.

There are five missionary stations, with a school attached to each, at Abbeokuta, and about the same number at Lagos. The congregations of these churches consist principally of people from Sierra Leone. There are many native pupils who also attend the services at the churches, but the number of adult converts is small, except as above remarked, from among the people from Sierra Leone.

All the people from Sierra Leone, as well as many of the natives speak English, and some also read and write correctly. I have seen at Abbeokuta several boys, who have never been out of that town, having a pretty correct knowledge of most of the branches of a common English education, English grammar, arithmetic, geography, etc., besides a good acquaintance with Scripture history. They make apt scholars.

4*

CHAPTER VIII

JOURNEY TO YORUBA.

Our Caravan—Atadi—Extortion of Carriers—Ilugun—Peter Elba—Open Air Accommodation—Articles left by the roadside for sale—Ijaye—Kumi—Telegraphic drums—Interview with Chief—"Palaver with the water"—Great Market—The Drivers—Carriers—Value of a Shirt—Departure for Oyo—Fever again—Visit to King Adelu—Exchange of Presents—Tax collecting—Snake-Charmer—Adeneji—Small Pox—Ogbomishaw—Dr. Delany, Fever still again—Scarcity of Water.

HAVING completed our business at Abbeokuta, we began to prepare for a journey through the entire extent of the Aku country, terminating at Ilorin, but were unable to carry out our intention for several weeks, owing to the illness of myself first, and my colleague next. At last we both found ourselves well, and after two or three days spent in purchasing horses, employing servants, carriers, and effecting other provisions, we finally left Abbeokuta at mid-day on the 16th January, 1860, for Ijaye. Our little caravan consisted of twelve persons, namely, of ourselves, two boys, one to the care of each horse, an interpreter, a cook, six carriers, besides several natives met on the road, who kept with us, as they were journeying in the same direction. The same evening we sojourned at Atadi, a small Egba town, where we were kindly accommodated by the "visitor" of the Church Missionary Society, a worthy, pious man, whose example and teachings are effecting much for those among whom he labors. He possesses a neat little house, which is very comfortable though built of mud and in the native style.

By daylight the next morning we expected to resume our journey, but were unable to obtain a relay of carriers for several hours; not that there were not several to be had, but finding that we were compelled to employ them, or be greatly incommoded, they seized the opportunity to exact more than three times the sum usually paid. Besides, they soon discovered that our interpreter, into whose hands all these things were committed, was a native of the coast, and therefore unacquainted with the manner of proceeding. There was no alternative but to submit to their extortion. No where are people quicker to perceive an advantage, and more ready to use it. We left Atadi about ten A.M. The road was exceedingly busy, as there were thousands of persons bearing palm-oil and other commodities to the coast for sale.

The next town at which we encamped for the night was Ilugun. When we were within five or six miles of it, one of our boys, Peter Elba, an intelligent sharp boy, who speaks English and reads and writes well, began to break down, his feet becoming sore and swollen, as he had never walked so much before. Tired of riding, I dismounted and placed the poor fellow on the horse the rest of the way. This was intended as much for my own accommodation as for his relief; nevertheless I never heard the last of it, as the poor fellow, deeply grateful for the act, told it to every body he met, either the interpreter or cook being generally near, to confirm or exaggerate his statements.

The headman of the little town having treated some missionaries unkindly, whether designedly or not I am unable to say, we were advised not to sojourn with him, but to pass through the town and put up at the house of an old man, living a short distance beyond the wall. We did so, as it is sometimes wise to take the advice of the missionaries. As soon as the headman learned that strangers had arrived, he sent a messenger desiring us to come to see him, which I did, accompanied by our interpreter, and was very kindly received. He could not present us a lamb or kid, because, said he, the young persons are not at home to catch them. This was equivalent to asking for a present, which I granted in the form of a tin box of matches, and a small looking-glass. He complained that both ourselves and other civilized persons passing through his town, had treated him ill, by not stopping at his house. I frankly explained the reason, namely, his unkind treatment of missionaries who had sojourned with him before. He protested that he had never designed any ill himself, and would not suffer his people to inflict any if he knew it. After all, I believe the whole matter was the result of misunderstanding, as he did not seem like one who would willingly harm any body, much less civilized people. Although the party with whom we sojourned had a large house, he really had no accommodation within it for travellers, so that we were compelled, as we have repeatedly done before and after, to sleep on a mat in the open air, where, however, being tired, we enjoyed a good repose, without any serious consequences. So much for the "pestilential night air of that baneful clime."

The next morning when we were ready to leave, poor Peter could not walk; so leaving some cowries for his expenses, we were obliged to leave him to come on with the mail-man, who was expected to pass in a few days. He reached Ijaye before we departed for the next town, Oyo, but was unable to accompany us further. We never saw him again, as on our return from the interior we were unable to enter the city which was surrounded by hostile forces. His abode with the missionaries is, however, a guarantee of his personal safety.

On the road to Ilugun we met in several places fruits and other articles exposed for sale, without any person near to watch them. There were several little heaps of cowries left by those who had purchased. A few cowries were also deposited near each article to indicate its price. It is incorrect to suppose, however, that these articles were entirely unprotected. Suspended from a rod there is a small bundle of dried grass—Shango's torch—hanging always over the articles for sale, which is an appeal to the god that he should set fire to the house of any one wicked enough to steal them. This is even a greater protection than the presence of a person could be, for there are those expert enough to elude human vigilance, who would never expect to do likewise to Shango.

Crossing what was then, in the dry season, a gentle brook, but which at other times is a river of considerable magnitude, we entered the gate of the city of Ijaye, and were conducted to the station of the American Baptists by a boy whom we met at the gate, dressed in a shirt of civilized manufacture, a sure indication that he was belonging to the "mission family." The occupants of the station, Messrs. Phillips and Stone, and the wife of the latter, were out at the time, but soon arrived, and invited us into the house. In a few minutes we were provided with as fine a supper as we ever enjoyed in Africa.

Ijaye is one of the largest of the Yoruba towns, containing not less than eighty thousand inhabitants. It is ruled by Kumi, entitled Arey, a man, intelligent, active, haughty, cruel, ambitious, stubborn and despotic, yet an excellent ruler, if we judge from the decorum of his people and the respect which they show him. By the people of the surrounding towns he is much hated, and will not be permitted to maintain his position longer than they can help. The town is a part of the Yoruba kingdom, but Kumi has for several years disputed the legitimacy and defied the authority of the king at Oyo, and has actually set up himself as his rival.

Accompanied by the missionaries mentioned before, we made his excellency a visit, a day or two after our arrival. He was not at home when we reached his palace, but his officials received us kindly, and promised to call him immediately, which one of them did by making a loud peculiar noise with a drum, which, with its drummer, is kept for this and similar purposes. These drummers can, we learned, communicate, nay, converse with each other at any distance within the sound of the instrument. After we were seated a few minutes the chief entered, attended by a large retinue, at the head of whom he walked with much grace and dignity. He seated himself in a piazza, the old men and officers of his court betook themselves to the left, the right side was reserved for us and our party, and the general crowd seated themselves promiscuously in front of us in the yard. Our interview was very cordial. We mentioned the object of our visit to the country, and obtained his consent, joyfully accorded, that our people should come to live in peace in his town, and he promised that they should have all the land they required. About to depart, I presented my hand to shake, which, forgetting himself, he was about to do, when the surprise of the missionaries and some other individuals of the crowd arrested him, and he drew back his hand. From superstitious motives, he never shakes hands with "Oyibos," but would have shaken ours, had it not been for the sensation exhibited at the time.

Several of the people of Ijaye lost their lives in the river, while fishing, which induced the Arey to make a law that no one should ever fish in that river again. He said that the river was angry because its children were killed, and therefore revenged itself by killing his children, as he calls his people. Liking the sport, but unwilling to break the law, the Rev. Mr. Phillips sent to request his permission to fish in the brook. He replied, that as long as neither he nor his people make any palaver with the water, the water could make no palaver with them, white man could do as he liked, but when the palaver came, he must keep it to himself.

The most noticeable feature of Ijaye is its market, covering an area of over twenty acres, and attended three times per week by from fifteen to twenty thousand persons. In it are found, besides native produce, commodities from almost every section of the globe: swords, sandals, silk-yarn, otto of rose, paper, beads, etc., from Egypt and other Mediterranean States of Africa; and cloths, cutlery, tin and earthen wares, guns, gunpowder, rum and tobacco, from England, the United States, France, Germany and the Brazils. Among the principal articles of native produce were sheep, goats, fowls, butter, Indian-corn or maize, rice, yams, (*Dioscorea Bulbifera,*) casava, (*Jatropha Janipha,*) sweet-potatoes, (*Convolvulus Batatas,*) Guinea-corn, (*Sorghum vulgare,*) beans, several varieties; cotton, raw and manufactured; clothing; mechanical and agricultural implements of iron, (native smelting;) brass, pewter and glass rings, and other trinkets, etc. As large and populous as is the market, it is conducted with the greatest order. There is a particular place appropriated for the sale of each class of goods: thus in one place may be seen spinners offering their yarn to those who weave; in another, weavers offering their cloths; then those who sell iron-ware, sitting in their own quarters, and next to them the dealers in beads and other ornaments: here is the meat-market, and there the wood-market, and the clothing-market, and the place for the sale of live-stock, etc. etc. One man manages the entire affair with the greatest ease. The same characteristics exist in all the other markets we visited from Lagos to Ilorin, but no where else were they so extensive.

We continued at Ijaye for a fortnight, spending the time in visiting the objects of interest in the neighborhood, taking photographic views, and otherwise making ourselves as comfortable as possible. On account of threatened hostilities between Ijaye and Oyo, the next town, we were unable to procure carriers when ready to resume our journey, and our interpreter, participating in the fears of the natives, would do little to help us in procuring them. We were finally obliged to go to seek them ourselves, in which we succeeded by lending each carrier a shirt, for so great is the respect entertained for the civilized, that even the assumption of the garb affords protection and the liberty of passing unmolested through a hostile country.

We were favored while at Ijaye with some fine opportunities for observing the peculiarities of the notorious *drivers*. These creatures are neither more nor less than ants, resembling nearly the black ants of this country, and identical with those of the West-Indies, where, however, they are less numerous. They are usually seen in countless myriads, marching in line with great order and apparent discipline. They never attack dwellings, except vermin or the like are suffered to accumulate; then they come, and usually again retire in a few hours, entirely ridding the place of the objects of their attack. Of course before these visitors the occupants of a room must retire: the only inconvenience is, that one is sometimes obliged to do this at midnight. The bite of a single ant is not very painful, but of course the same can not be said of twenty or thirty simultaneous nips on different parts of the person. The inducement to dance is then irresistible. They never leave their line of march to attack an object not molesting them. I have myself stooped over a large train for an hour, watching their progress. The instant you touch them, however, fifty or sixty of the largest and most formidable dart off towards you, when a retreat is prudent. Immediately they return to the line again. It is curious to observe their tactics in attacking larger animals, a rat for instance. A single ant attaches itself to it: the poor creature naturally stops to rid itself of the paltry aggressor, but this delay enables others to join in the attack: for a few minutes a desperate combat is waged, and many an ant, persistently retaining its grasp on the flanks of the victim, is parted asunder by the effort to detach it. Overcome chiefly by fatigue from its own vigorous exertions, the rat at length passively resigns itself to the voracity of its assailants, making now and then only a convulsive effort indicative of the extreme torture to which it is subjected. An effectual way of ridding an apartment of them is to fill the mouth with salt, and when it is moistened with saliva, to blow it over them. They then hasten away with great precipitation. It is not the salt, but the saliva, I think, which is offensive to them, for once at Ijaye, unable to procure salt, I took water into my mouth, and after it was well mixed with the secretion I blew it out at them with the same effect as if salt was used.

It is obvious that while these curious creatures are occasionally the cause of some inconvenience, they are also the instrument of much good, in destroying vermin, which in such a climate might otherwise become intolerable. I never saw or heard of a bed-bug in Africa, their absence being doubtless due to the aggressions of the *drivers*.

On the 4th February we left Ijaye for Oyo, from five to seven hours' journey, in a north-eastern direction. For the two or three days preceding I was troubled with an attack of bilious fever, from which I fancied myself free, but in less than two hours after leaving, it returned with great violence; nevertheless I continued the journey, but was exceedingly ill when I reached Oyo, so as to have given our kind friend the Rev. Mr. Reed, of the American Baptist Mission, whose house was our home, a great deal of trouble. The next day I was better, and by a timely administration of remedies continued well all the rest of our sojourn in Africa. Here we met Mr. Meeking, of the Church Mission Society, a very worthy young man, whom we must here heartily thank for his many kind offices. Accompanied by these gentlemen and interpreters, we made a visit to Adelu, the king of the Yoruba nation, who welcomed us very cordially to his town. There is not another chief or king in the whole Aku country who is surrounded by more of the circumstances befitting his rank, than this man. His compound, or if you please, his palace, is the largest in the country, accommodating over fifteen hundred persons—wives, children, slaves, etc. The number of his wives is said to be fully one thousand. Many of these, however, are only nominally so, for according to a custom among them, the wives of a father at his death become the wives of his son, and frequently we find very old women calling themselves, on account of the position in society it gives them, the wives of one or other of the kings or chiefs, who in reality were only the wives of the grandfathers of such.

It was necessary to send a messenger the day before, to announce to Fufu, the king's lieutenant, our intended visit to his majesty, as, because we were strangers he would only receive us in state, and required due notice to effect the necessary preparations. He was seated under an *acabi*, one of the turret-like arrangements already mentioned, surrounded by his wives, his head reclining on one, his feet resting on another; one fanned him, another wiped the perspiration from his face; one held an umbrella of many colors over his head, and another a small vessel carefully covered up, in which his majesty occasionally deposited his salivary secretions,* which accumulated fast in consequence of the quantity of snuff he takes in the

---

* They have a superstition that their enemies can hurt them by procuring their spittle and subjecting it to certain manipulations.

mouth, in common with all the native adults, and often even the children of this region. His dress consisted of a costly tobe and shocoto of the same pattern, both nicely embroidered, a cap of red silk-velvet, and Mohammedan sandals. On his wrists he wore màssive silver rings, and a strand of large corals about his neck.

In front of the acabi, on both sides of a passage left by which to approach his majesty, were several of his slaves, the principal officers of his household, several men with long trumpets, on which they blew loud blasts, applauding those points of the conversation deemed wise or witty, and several eunuchs.

As usual, we explained the object of our visit to Africa, with which he was as much pleased as any of the other native authorities with whom we had before treated. We made him a small present, and received according to custom a return present of a fine sheep and three beads of cowries. Our interview was an exceedingly pleasant one, and every day we continued at Oyo after that, a messenger was sent to inquire after the health of the king's relatives, as he ever after called us.*

A tax was being collected for the expense of the war which the king was preparing against Ijaye, the

---

* See page 38.

manner of collecting which we had an opportunity of observing. It was very simple. At each of the gates, which are only wide enough to suffer a horse to pass easily, there stood two men, one on each side, elevated on blocks of wood, who as the people passed through returning from their farms, abstracted from the baskets a few yams, ears of corn, or of whatever else their loads consisted.

One day in going through the market we saw a man sitting by the way-side, to whom many people as they passed gave a few cowries. As we approached nearer we found that he was one of the celebrated snake-charmers, and had at the time one of these reptiles about his neck and body as large as a man's arm : of the length we could not well judge, as much of it was coiled under his garment.

My other boy, Adeneji, here took the small-pox, and of course could not accompany us further. We left Oyo on the 8th February, and two days after arrived at Ogbomishaw, at which we sojourned only one day. We visited the chief, informed him of the object of our visit, exchanged presents, took an excursion over the town, and left early the next morning. Except a fine park, we found no object of interest peculiar to this town. Although a large place, of fully fifty thousand inhabitants, there were no missionaries.

The American Baptists have a fine station there, but no missionary has occupied it for more than a year. There is no impediment whatever, and it seems a pity that it should be left thus uncared for.

Early in the morning of the 10th February, we left Ogbomishaw for Ilorin, the terminus of our journey. On account of the difficulty of procuring carriers, we were compelled to wait at the gate until nearly four in the afternoon. In the mean time Dr. Delany began to experience symptoms of returning fever; nevertheless, as it was necessary to hasten our journey, he persisted in going. We had not left two hours when the symptoms became so aggravated that he was obliged to dismount and lie by the road-side. Leaving our cook with him, I rode on as fast as possible, to find a place at which we could sojourn for the night, and fortunately found a small farm village about four miles further on. I then rode back, and met him about two miles from where he was left.

It was, fortunately for us, the dry season, when it is really more comfortable to sleep in the open air, which notwithstanding the Doctor's health we were obliged to do, as there were no accommodations for us under shelter. We left early the next morning to reach Ilorin, one long day's journey from this village. It was perhaps the most uncomfortable day's journey we ever had, as we could not procure a draught of clean water, the brooks and springs being almost all dry, except here and there a little pool so stagnant, dirty and nauseous that only severe thirst induced us to touch it. This was, however, a trouble that could easily have been provided against, by each party taking a small bottle of this necessary liquid for his own use.

Within three or four miles of Ilorin we rested at a farm-village to change carriers, etc., and take each of us, horses and all, a long draught of water, under such circumstances an invaluable luxury.

CHAPTER IX.

ILORIN.

Magnificent Conflagration—Grassy Plains and Forests—Freedom of the Country from Beasts and Reptiles; why—Extravagant Welcome—Nasamo the Executioner, and his Dwelling—Wifeless—Royal Present of Food—Prisoners—Interview with the King—Schools—Arabians—Mulatto—Musical Instruments—Banjo—Beggars—Looms—Gambari Market—Escort.

THERE was just light enough to enable us to see the dim outline of the walls as we approached Ilorin, and by the time we were within the gates it was dark, but the atmosphere was illumined by a brilliant light from the burning of grass in the plain to the right of the city—a magnificent spectacle. Except between Abbeokuta and Ijaye, where there is a dense forest through which it requires fully five hours to pass, forming the division between the territory of the Egbas and Yorubas, the country is clear, with only low scrubby trees much scattered, with an undergrowth of rank tall grass. In some places, from what cause it is difficult to say, there can be found no other kinds of vegetation than this grass, particularly in the neighborhood of large cities. Every year, after the harmattan winds, the natives set fire to it, causing an immense conflagration, sweeping over the country like a tornado.

From the mission-house at Ijaye, southward over an elevated country without the gate, we have seen a line of fire fully a mile long, driven by the wind so furiously as to entirely clear a space of ten or fifteen square miles in less than two hours, and still progressing out of sight, making a terrible noise. As it burns, thousands of birds and other small animals are driven out, and are immediately seized by hawks, which during the dry season are very abundant. It is from these fires, doubtless, that there is so little forest land and so few wild beasts, serpents, etc., in this country. During the whole time we were in Africa we saw only three living serpents, one about the neck of the man near the market at Oyo, one at Abbeokuta, and a small, but they say a very venomous one, on the road towards Isehin, where I also saw a few fine deer, which are always expert enough to get out of the way of these fires. We also saw a fawn bounding at full speed over the plain near Ilorin. The fire which so beautifully illumined the darkness as we entered the city was of the kind above referred to.

We met at the gate quite a concourse of persons,

chiefly women, who gave us an extravagant welcome, and brought food and water. We partook of the latter only, and hastened to the house of Nasamo, the sheriff or public executioner, to which we were directed by the advice of the Rev. Mr. Reid, who had not long before visited Ilorin. His dwelling, at no time adapted to the purposes of hospitality, was still worse now that a recent fire in his neighborhood had compelled him, as well as all his neighbors, to remove the thatch from his roof. The entire building and grounds were comprised in an area of not over thirty feet square, and this space accommodated, with ourselves, more than eighteen persons, besides our horses. Nasamo, though evidently not less than seventy or eighty years old, is yet vigorous both in mind and physical constitution. He was the first important personage we met without a single wife: he had one who made him the father of three or four daughters, but since her death he has lived a widower. One of his daughters attends to his domestic affairs,

Early the following day we sent our interpreter to salute the king, and inform him of our visit to his capital, asking to be permitted as soon as possible to pay our respects to him in person. The interpreter was conducted to Dungari, the king's prime-minister, who received, and conveyed the message to his master.

Shortly after we received a return salutation from his majesty, together with a large vessel of well-prepared native food, sufficient to feed both ourselves, and attendants for the day, also a similar present from Dungari. These presents were continued for the whole time we remained in the town, but after three or four days our servants and the other inmates of the compound retained, and consumed it among themselves, without even informing us of its arrival, a liberty we cheerfully granted for several reasons.

Every day we were requested to prepare to visit the king, but were continually put off with some slight excuse till the fourth day, when we were led into his presence. This unnecessary delay occasioned us considerable inconvenience, for we were in the mean time virtually prisoners, not being permitted to go out of our uncomfortable quarters until we had first seen his majesty, and obtained his gracious consent to see the town; and even after this consent was obtained, we were only permitted to go out accompanied by Nasamo. The excuse for this was, that he would protect us from harm by the people, a poor excuse, as we had not the least cause of fear, every one being remarkably civil and respectful towards us.

Our interview with his majesty, King Shita, was very interesting. Quite unexpectedly he permitted us

at this first interview to see his face, a privilege he
never accorded publicly to any who had before visited
the place, at the same time informing us, that it was
because he regarded us as his own people, descendants
of native Africans. Besides the direct subject of our
mission, we conversed on the forms of civilized government, his majesty asking many questions respecting
Queen Victoria, and the ruler of the country from
which we came, of whom the American missionaries
had before informed him. As a "ruse," he invited us
to accompany him to his mosque, to which he said he
was just going. We accepted his invitation, but when
we prepared to go, he laughed and again seated himself, saying that he was glad we seemed to have no
prejudices against his religion; he was seated on a mat
in a long piazza, usually entirely screened, but on this
occasion the screens were drawn up just where he sat,
so as to expose him to view, but still keeping out of
sight many of his wives. He is an old man, and like
the king of Abbeokuta has had the misfortune to lose
an eye. He is not a pure Negro, but like many of the
Fulanees in his town, one of his parents, most likely
his father, must have been an Arabian; his physiognomy therefore is not purely Negro. He is a man of
small stature, but well proportioned, and was neatly at-

tired in a white tobe, turban, and red cap. He was surrounded by a number of well-dressed men, priests, officers of his court, eunuchs, etc., all of whom sat in a clean sheltered space before his piazza, but on the ground. We were placed about four yards in front of him, to the right of the company, except Dungari, who with our interpreter was on the right of us. Although the king understands Aku well, and therefore could converse directly with our interpreter, yet the customs of his court require, that all that is said be communicated to him in Fulanee by Dungari, who as before remarked, (see page 61) is, except the king, the most important personage of Ilorin. He is by birth a Fulanee, but of the blackest type of Negroes, as are indeed ninety-five per cent of them; those who are lighter in complexion, or differ in physiognomic conformation, being more or less of Arabian intermixture. In common with many of the people he reads and writes Arabic, to teach which, there are quite a number of schools in the town. We saw there, in the market-places chiefly, several Arabians, some of whom had travelled immense distances across the continent, for purposes of trade, in which they all engage. Other travellers speak of "white people" in Ilorin, but although we spent as long a time there as perhaps any traveller had done, we were unable to find a single individual even as light as myself, though of twenty-five per cent negro blood.

One girl about twelve years old was met, who was evidently the child of some slave-trader of the coast, as she was certainly a mulatto whose father was a white man and not an Arabian, than whom she was much lighter in complexion. Every person in Ilorin is said to speak both the Aku and Fulanee languages, and we found no exception among those who were not foreigners.

The musical instruments of the people of Ilorin more nearly resemble those used in civilized countries, than those seen in other sections of Africa nearer the coast. In a large band which performed before the palace, there were several wind instruments, two or three of which were like our clarionets, and others resembled an English postman's trumpet. An old man came to play and sing for us very often. The instrument he used was the exact counterpart of the Banjo, only smaller, but played in the same way and producing similar music. Accompanied by our *soi-disant* jailer, we made several excursions through the town. Except the existence of numerous mosques and markets, there is no material difference in the appearance of it from others.

There were plenty of blind beggars, a sight quite unusual in other African towns, where we seldom ever saw a beggar. They are attracted to the place doubtless from the custom among the Mohammedans, (a religious custom,) of often ostentatiously distributing money among them.

As an example of the extent to which cotton fabrics are manufactured, we encountered one day in a ride of less than an hour more than one hundred and fifty weavers, busily employed at their looms. These weavers are seen also in the other towns, where they were formerly as abundant, but the influx of better and cheaper fabrics from England has very nearly superseded the necessity of them.

To the Gambari market, allusion has already been made as the greatest depot for the sale of slaves, besides which, there were exposed for sale fine horses, donkeys, mules, horse-trappings, swords, leather work, silk clothing, tobes, antimony, salt, cola nuts, stationery, etc. etc.

Tobacco is much cultivated by the people of Ilorin. They do not cure it like the Americans.

The day before we departed we received a special invitation to exhibit our curiosities—my watch, fowling-piece, etc.—to the king, which gave him much pleasure, and induced the remark from Dungari: "Verily, if I had not a strong mind, I would embrace the customs and religion of such a people."

The next day we took leave of the king, who made us a second fine present of two mats, two pairs of beautifully wrought sandals, and three heads of cowries "to pay our expenses down." At our first interview, after receiving ours, he had made us a present of equal value. A horseman and two foot-soldiers were sent with us, as an escort, and quite a multitude followed us out of the town, wishing us a safe journey and blessings of every kind. The people of Ilorin are not all Mussulmans, there being also a large, almost equal proportion of Yorubas, heathens; these, headed by a powerful Balagun, occasion King Shita considerable trouble, and might one day remove him and his party from power, an object openly avowed. We saw a large number of convicts about the streets, their legs chained so as to permit them a very limited and peculiar locomotion. Such prisoners are not found in other towns, being either sold into foreign slavery or decapitated as the penalty for their offense—the former, a kind of punishment the teachings of their religion forbid the Mohammedans inflicting on their own people.

CHAPTER X

RETURN

"Two horsemen," and their adventure—Exchange horses—What about Vaughn—Progress arrested—New route—Voices in the bush—Village in Ashes—Isehin—A Hunting-Party—Dead man by the Roadside — Ibadan Soldiers, another adventure—"Enough, Enough, white man, go on!"—A city on a hill—Berecadu, and its defenses—Night travel in Africa—Abbeokuta again—"The Dahomians are coming"—Deputation—The Doctor is come, and how he did it—Final Departure for the Coast—The Carrier Nuisance once more—Troubles—Heroic Woman—Safe at Lagos—Departure—Kru Men—A Slaver.

ON the morning of the third day after our departure from Ilorin we reached Ogbomishaw, where we intended to remain only that day, to rest, and proceed early the next, as we were anxious to reach the coast to obtain our letters; but we were disappointed, as no carriers would stir out of the town on account of the hostilities raging amongst the people of Oyo, Ibadan, and Ijaye.

Having spent the day in fruitless search for carriers, we had just returned to the house, which, through the kindness of the American Baptist Missionaries, we were permitted to occupy, when two horsemen rode up to the door, and dismounting, entered, weary, starved and almost in rags.

These were the Rev Mr. Stone, and a colored American carpenter in the employ of the missionaries. The surprise of seeing them so unexpectedly, and under such distressing circumstances, being somewhat allayed, Mr. Stone briefly related to us his adventures as follows:

A colored man named Vaughn, an American, had selected for his abode a locality about three hours' journey from the city of Ijaye, on the road towards Ibadan. The Arey ascertaining that the Ibadans were moving against him, sent information to the missionaries, that they should go and bring their friend within the city, otherwise he could not answer for his safety. Mr. Stone, accompanied by Russel, almost immediately set out on horseback to apprise Vaughn of his danger, and persuade him to come with them. The horse on which Mr. Stone rode, was purchased some months before from the Arey, and was well known all through the country as his favorite war-horse; he was one of the largest, and except that the infirmities of age were becoming manifest, one of the handsomest among the Yoruba horses; besides, only a few weeks before, two large, warlike, Mexican saddles were received from

America, which the horses wore at the time of the adventure. They progressed on their journey unmolested until they reached the house of Vaughn, and unfortunately found it already entirely deserted, with much of his property destroyed, and scattered over the ground. There was every indication that the enemy was there and that something serious had befallen their friend. Nevertheless they concluded to proceed to the next village, about one hour's ride, to ascertain, if possible, his fate. They had progressed a few miles when they encountered a body of Ibadans who commanded them to halt and remain with them until the Balagun of the party arrived. Our friends, presuming on the respect always shown to civilized men, and the virtue of the horses, thought fit to disregard the injunction, and giving reins and spurs to their steeds would certainly have soon left the Ibadans far in the rear, had not suddenly before them, and on every side, a large number of soldiers, like spectres made their unwelcome appearance, and actually pointed their long guns at the fugitives, and would have fired, had they not immediately abandoned their design of so unceremoniously forsaking their company. Some, indignant at their attempt to escape, would have done them bodily injury but for the interference of their superiors. After all, they were pretty roughly used, their clothes torn, their hats stolen. There was no alternative, so they passively submitted.

In a few minutes the Balagun arrived, and sent the captives in charge of a few armed men to Ibadan. Arriving there, they were immediately taken before Ogumola, the chief of the city, who after much questioning, suffered them to depart. The timely interference of the Rev. Mr. Hinderer of the Church Mission, stationed at Ibadan, conduced much to their being dismissed with so little trouble. The circumstance of Mr. Stone's riding Arey's war-horse, looking, as well as the other horse, so martial in his caparison, induced the soldiers to regard him and his companion as spies, and hence the cause of their capture; and it was only after good evidence was afforded, that the horse was purchased from the Arey, and also that their mission without the walls of Ijaye was a peaceable one, that they were dismissed.

Not wishing to return by the same road, they attempted to pass through Iwo and Oyo, to Ijaye, but arriving at Iwo, they learned that the road to Oyo was in possession of soldiers who would not suffer any one to pass; on this account they were obliged to proceed to Ogbomishaw. They arrived as before narrated, hungry, tired, and pitifully distressed in mind, particularly Mr. Stone, on account of his wife, who must have suffered extreme agony from the apprehension that harm had overtaken her husband.

Not wishing again to be annoyed on account of the horse, Mr. Stone offered to exchange him for mine, a fine young animal, but not worth in money-value more than half his, to which I consented, as, being well known to the King of Oyo, I could take the horse into his capital without suspicion of connection with the rebel chief.

The next day we heard that some Egba traders were expected at the farm-village near Ogbomishaw, and that their carriers, who would have to return thence to Oyo, would be glad of the job of taking our parcels thither. I immediately went off to the village, and had the good fortune to engage them. I then hurried back to Ogbomishaw, and having completed our preparations, the next morning we were on the way to Oyo. Mr. Stone, in order I suppose to get as far as possible from association with the animal, rode ahead of us, so as to reach that place a day before us.

We never met a single living soul on the road to Oyo, several thriving villages being now quite deserted, the inhabitants taking refuge in the larger towns.

We arrived at Oyo early on Sunday morning, and proceeded to the compound of the Rev. Mr. Reid, of the American Baptist Mission, whom we did not find, as both he and Mr. Meeking, of the Church Missionary Society, accompanied by a messenger from the king, had gone to Ibadan, to seek Mr. Stone, who had arrived on Saturday evening, and, expecting us, had kindly ordered breakfast, of which, with a keen appetite, we were just about to partake, when Mr. Reid also rode up to the door. He did not go all the journey to Ibadan, having been informed at Iwo that the object of his search was safe and had gone to Ogbomishaw, thence to reach Oyo. Mr. Stone immediately after breakfast set out for Ijaye, to relieve as soon as possible the distress which his wife and friends endured on his account.

As for Vaughn, the party whom Mr. Stone had gone to seek, a few days before he had procured from Ibadan a number of men to assist him to remove his things into that town: unfortunately he got into a quarrel with some of these, one of whom struck him a blow on the head with his weapon, wounding him severely: he returned the blow, and leaving the man apparently dead, fled to Ibadan. Except his money, and a few other articles of value which he had before secured, he lost all his property by this adventure.

We continued at Oyo more than a week, not being able to procure carriers for our parcels. We could have gone on ourselves without any fear of harm, but it was impossible to leave all our things : it was at the same time essential to reach the coast within a month, as our funds were insufficient for a longer stay. After some consultation, it was determined that I should make an effort to get to Abbeokuta down the valley of the Ogun through Isehin.

Accordingly, leaving all the parcels in the care of the Doctor, taking with me only the means of living on the journey, and accompanied by our cook and interpreter, the latter to return for the Doctor if carriers could be found, we left Oyo on the morning of the 6th of March, and arrived at Isehin about eight o'clock the same evening. The road, at best but little frequented, was now completely deserted, and in many places almost impassable on horseback. Two or three hours from Oyo, we came to the iron-smelting village already referred to.

It was apparently entirely unoccupied, and I dismounted and examined the construction of their furnaces: remounting and again attempting to go forward, my attendants hesitated, declaring they heard voices in the bush ahead.

I affected to despise their fears, and moved forwards, bidding them follow, which they did at a very respectful distance. True, we had not advanced a hundred yards when we perceived several groups of armed men on both sides of the road a little way ahead: as we approached, they directed their weapons towards us in rather a threatening manner, yet they did not seem hostile; so urging my horse to a brisk trot, I rode amongst them, laughing and cheerfully saluting them as I approached. They could not help laughing too, but when I presented my hand successively to the first three or four, neither would touch it: passing the others, I presented it somewhat insistingly to one who seemed the leader: he shook it, several others following his example. They merely inquired whence we came, and suffered us to pass.

About two hours after, we crossed the Ogun and suddenly encountered one of the saddest spectacles in Africa, a village only a few days before full of life and activity, now entirely depopulated, its inhabitants captured as slaves, itself in ruins and ashes. The people belonged to Oyo, and were collected there on account of the employment of ferrying passengers over the Ogun during the rainy season. The King of Oyo having a short time before captured a few of the people of Ijaye, Arey in retaliation sent an expedition against the place, and suddenly pouncing upon the unsuspecting inhabitants at midnight, took every individual and burnt the place.

During this day's journey we saw the largest number of wild animals, deer, monkeys, etc., especially near the river; and as we passed through the village we perceived a flock of Guinea-hens covering an area of over an acre. As before mentioned, we arrived at Isehin about eight in the evening. Mr. Elba, the native reader of the Church Mission, and father of the boy already mentioned, kindly afforded us accommodation. We tarried long enough the next day to pay our respects to the king. We found his majesty attired in his hunting costume, horses, attendants, dogs and arms, all ready to depart, consequently he could not afford a lengthy audience, but was very courteous, and presented me a small smoked animal not unlike the armadillo, a present, I was told, significant of much respect, but which I could not sufficiently appreciate, particularly as it partook of the qualities of venison when most acceptable to certain palates. We also called on the chief Balagun, who gave us a hearty welcome and a few dried fishes. The number of inhabitants does not exceed twenty thousand, and the town is one of the only two in this section, Iwo being the other, which have existed before the troubles which led to the formation of Ijaye, Abbeokuta, etc. We left Isehin about eleven A.M., and reached Awaye, the next town, the same evening.

The road was quiet and deserted, the people every where fearing to leave home on account of the unsettled condition of affairs. There was the body of a man near the road, a mile from the town, where it had lain for more than a week. A few of a straggling party of Ijaye soldiers lurking in the neighborhood, having unsuccessfully pursued some farmers, were returning to their companions, who fired on them, mistaking them for the fugitives, and unfortunately killed one. The chief ordered that his body, which of course his companions had no time either to take away or bury, should remain, as a lesson to similar marauding parties.

Not more than half an hour after our arrival, the chief waited on me in person to salute me and welcome me to his town. He is the youngest chief in the Aku country, but certainly one of the most intelligent, to judge by his conversation. He sent me a large bowl of milk for supper, and the next morning a fine pig, although he knew I was not in a position to make him a return present. He was very anxious that some civilized person should come to live in his town. It is strange that while, including teachers and catechists, a place like Abbeokuta should have ten or twelve missionaries, besides an indefinite number of native readers or visitors, there should be only an ignorant visitor, whose sole qualification is his ability to read, allowed to a town of from sixteen to twenty thousand people.

My horse and men being tired, we rested all the next day at Awaye.

A woman with her son and daughter besought me to permit them to go under our protection to Abbeokuta. I told her she was welcome to all the protection I could afford, and we left together the next morning early. At about eleven o'clock, when halfway on our journey to Bi-olorun-pellu, we suddenly met about two hundred Ibadan soldiers. My servants, who were before me, attempted to pass by the foremost of them, but were very roughly arrested. Myself and the rest of the party soon came up and were all immediately surrounded. They kept us, while discussing the fate of my people, for nearly two hours. At length they demanded a present as the condition on which they would allow us to proceed. I had nothing to give, having left Oyo with only two suits of clothes, one on my back, the other in a small bundle. My other things consisted only of a gutta-percha sheet and some cooking utensils. I told the man who carried them to open the things and allow them to take whatever they desired: seeing we had nothing, they informed my interpreter, after a little consideration among themselves, that we could depart peaceably, but they must keep as their captives the woman and her two children. It was too distressing to see three human beings about to be deprived of their liberty. The old woman wept bitterly, but her tears were apparently unheeded. I told them that it was impossible for me to leave these people; they had placed themselves under my protection, therefore I could not permit them to be taken away, except with myself also; that they could take my horse, my watch, my money, all I had, in short; but I would not permit them to take these people. They hesitated, I saw they were moved, and I kept up my entreaties. At length the balagun or captain, to whom I addressed myself, and who remained silent all the time I spoke, with almost a tear in his eye, exclaimed, " *Oto, oto, oyibo, molo !* " " Enough, enough, white man, go on." When one of his party attempted to take away a tin cup my interpreter carried, he drew his sword, declaring that it was at the peril of any one to touch us. Some of his people seemed much disappointed. We hurried away, and four hours after were climbing an immense rock, rising like an island from the surrounding plain, on the summit of which is situated " Biolorun-pellu," "*If the Lord wills.*"

The party we had so fortunately escaped from, belonged to the same who had arrested the Rev. Mr. Stone, for they knew the horse, and two or three of them contended that he was the same, while others more skilled in logic showed that it was impossible, for the reasons that he was sent to Ibadan, that he was not ridden by the same oyibo, and that he had not on the same saddle. The argument was conclusive, so they contended no longer; but there seemed to be still a few who, by an occasional shake of the head as they viewed the animal, continued to indicate a lingering skepticism. The horse, in his turn, seemed to recognize his old acquaintances, and looked all the time as suspicious as possible.

The people of this town, like those of Abbeokuta, flying from place to place before a relentless enemy, had at last betaken themselves to this naturally impregnable position, and in view of its safety called it, "Bi-olorun-pellu," for, said they, only by the Lord's will, and not by the power of man, can we be removed hence. I never perhaps endured greater labor than in the effort to get my horse up the almost inaccessible cliffs, although assisted by our party, even the women; and when at last we succeeded, the poor beast was much bruised. There are only two passes into the town, one by which it is entered from Isehin, and the other from Berecadu. Three men at each of these could successfully defend the place against any number. It could also hold out against a long siege, for not only is there always a supply of provisions stored away to last for at least two years, but the interstices of the rocks and other places unattainable except by the inhabitants, are susceptible of cultivation, although the amount of produce thus obtained would hardly be equivalent to their ordinary consumption. The same evening we arrived I called to pay my respects to the chief, from whom I received the usual kind treatment: he presented me, as did the chief of Awaye, with a fine pig. The Balagun also gave me a large "rooster." I left the next morning with a thousand blessings from the people, for the woman who with her children I had aided in saving from slavery, had told the matter to all her friends, as she did also at Berecadu and at Abbeokuta, and they, with all the warm gratitude of the African's nature, were exceedingly lavish in their acknowledgments of the deed.

We arrived at Berecadu on the evening of the same day, without any incidents on the journey worth recording. At one of the crossings of the Ogun, we met a large company of Ibadan soldiers, again lurking like wild beasts to seize any unsuspecting native who in such times should venture out to their farms. They had taken possession of a few huts on the banks of the river, used in the wet season by those who make a business of crossing passengers on large calabashes as already described.

First one, evidently the balagun, came out and saluted us very kindly, then another, and still another, until there were more than thirty standing around us. I strove to appear myself, quite at ease, and shook hands and joked with them, but the woman and her son and daughter gave them a "wide berth," while the interpreter and cook, the latter of whom I shall better call Johnson, could ill repress their fears, although they behaved well.

Berecadu is a town of about thirty or thirty-five thousand inhabitants, judging from the extent and character of its only market. The people are partly Yorubas and partly Egbas, paying tribute to both nations, but obliged to guard against both also, as each seems determined to compel the paying of tribute to itself alone. Its defenses are so well contrived that it would almost be as difficult a place to take as Biolorun-pellu, except by surprise, and this is not likely, as a large number of armed men, "keepers of the city," are stationed every night at the gates.

There are two walls encompassing the whole city, leaving a space of about two hundred yards between them, and this space contains a dense forest, with an interlacing undergrowth, utterly impassable to an enemy except by the use of means incompatible with the dispatch of warfare.

We sojourned with the Visitor, who lives in the compound of the chief, to whom I as usual paid my respects and explained the object of my visit. He is almost the most miserable person of the town, old, blind, neglected and in dirt and rags, yet cheerful and apparently much concerned for his people. There is a second chief or regent, who is charged with the municipal administration.

Leaving Berecadu shortly after midnight, we arrived at Abbeokuta in time for breakfast. Except in the warmest part of the day, it is always pleasant to travel in Africa, but it is particularly so at night or near day-break: the country then seen by the mellow light of the moon, or by the gray twilight, seems twice as wild and magnificent, and the flowers distill their perfume in greater abundance: now and then, it is true, one hears the dismal screech of some night-bird, or the yell or howl of some small animal disturbed in his repose by intruding footsteps, but these serve only to break the monotony; and besides, there are the gentle cooing of doves, and the cheerful voices and merry laughter of your native attendants, sufficient to cheer any heart.

Whenever it was practicable, we always preferred travelling at such times; and although much is said in disparagement of night air in Africa, certainly in our case, if injurious at all, it was not as much so as the effects of the sun.

We found Abbeokuta in considerable commotion. Only a few days before, the Dahomians were known to be advancing against the city, but informed doubtless by their spies of the reception that was prepared for them, they suddenly wheeled about and retraced their steps, not without committing much depredation among the people through whose territory they passed.

Every one was also speculating on the war in the interior, and its probable consequences and duration. Being the only person who had returned thence for a fortnight, every one wanted to hear news from me: the king and chiefs desired an interview particularly, respecting the Ibadans we met on the road, who were suspected to be loitering there to join the Dahomians in their contemplated attack.

The morning after my arrival I was waited upon at the house of my kind friend Mr. Samuel Crowther, Jr., by a large deputation of the relatives of the woman who came with me from Awaye. She was not with them herself, being ill from the effect of her fright and the fatigue of such hurried travelling; but there were the son and daughter and her other children, brothers, sisters, aunts, uncles, cousins, and their husbands, wives, children, etc. They brought with them presents of chickens, eggs, fruits, cola-nuts and many other suitable gifts.

The interpreter had accompanied me with the object of returning to inform the Doctor whether carriers could be obtained on the route, and if so, to come with him and our luggage after me to Abbeokuta; but the condition of the road, as the reader already knows, rendered it impossible even for the interpreter to return alone.

My next plan was to return myself, taking with me the letter-bags of the missionaries, which they were very anxious to receive; but both the interpreter and Johnson, who belonged to Lagos, wanted to go home, the former because his mother was at the point of death, the latter because he was longing to see his wife, but he promised to return in a week, and to indicate his sincerity refused to take his wages until then. True to his word, he came at the appointed time, and we were about to set out the next morning, my horse waiting, when our native boy Adeneje, who was left at Oyo with small-pox, came in with a note from my colleague informing me that he had just arrived at our usual place of abode at the Baptist Mission House. After making several fruitless efforts to procure carriers, he was at length favored by the king with the protection of a detachment of soldiers going to join the Ibadans against Kumi, Arey of Ijaye, a few of them being also detailed to the duty of carriers, an office they seemed to regard as derogatory to the dignity of soldiers, judging from the trouble they gave him. The king also sent with him a special messenger to indicate that he was the king's friend, and as such should receive proper consideration. He made the journey through Iwo and Ibadan. When he arrived at the latter place he could only procure carriers for a portion of our things, the Rev. Mr. Hinderer, with whom the Doctor sojourned at Ibadan, kindly consenting to take care of the rest for us. The reader will remember that we had already left a large portion of our property at Ijaye, which though safe, we could not procure, as we were unable to enter the city. From both these circumstances we lost most of our collections, and also some fine photographs.

By the first of April we had completed our arrangements, and were to leave on the morning of the third for Lagos. Carriers were engaged for the journey, as we intended to travel by land, it being the dry season; but when the time arrived we were as usual put off and annoyed by their unconquerable love of gain, and desire to make if possible a fortune out of us. They would come, examine the parcels, and charge three or four times more than the labor was worth. One refuses to pay, and they walk off. After great trouble you procure another set; they serve you in the same way; then the first return and abate somewhat, but the charge is still too great, and you refuse to pay it; they walk off again, expecting that as you are in a hurry, you will call them back, which of course you do not, having acquired some wisdom by your past experience in the country. They go out of sight for twenty minutes, and at last return again, asking an honest price, and the bargain is completed. Surviving all the annoyance, which I assure the reader is much worse than I can depict, we at length left Abbeokuta about nine o'clock in the evening on the fifth of April, intending to sleep that night at Aro, and depart early the next morning; but having attained that point, our relentless carriers placed down their loads, and declared that as they were heavy they would not carry them any further without more pay. This they did because the next day being Oro-day, it would be impossible to get others, and we could not delay a day longer without the risk of losing our passage to England. I was at a loss what to do, but of all things I would not submit to their extortion. At last Mr. Pedro, an intelligent young native, kindly volunteered to procure a canoe to take down the things, thus enabling us to dispense with the carriers entirely. After some effort he succeeded. It was then concluded that the Doctor, accompanied by Johnson, should proceed by land, while I should go with the canoe to look after the safety of our things. The Doctor left about ten o'clock A.M., the things were placed on board, my horse sent back to Abbeokuta, and stepping into the canoe it was pushed off. We proceeded with much labor for about two miles, when it was found impossible to go further: there was not enough water to float it. We were then left in a worse dilemma than at first, for a little more pay would have secured the services of the carriers. Leaving the canoe, I returned to Aro, to procure if possible the aid of a man to push it on, and fortunately met Messrs. Josiah Crowther and Faulkner, the latter a respectable young man from Sierra Leone, who seeing and pitying my unlucky position, sent a few of their laborers to take the luggage down to Agbamiya, a point further down the river, from which place there is always enough water to float a loaded canoe. These laborers instead of returning with the things to Aro, and proceeding thence by the direct road, attempted a short cut and went three or four miles out of the way, so that we never arrived at Agbamiya until about six in the afternoon. Arriving there, by a little more trouble and the offer of good pay on condition of leaving that night, I procured another canoe, and away we went at last.

There is always trouble travelling in Africa with luggage, but it is far less in the interior than among the semi-civilized, neither Christian nor heathen, natives of the coast, who acquiring all the vices of the white man, know little and practise still less of his virtues.

I never experienced real hardship until in this little journey between Abbeokuta and the coast. No sooner had we fairly started than it began to rain heavily, and it continued raining more or less until we reached Lagos, so that, sleeping and waking, I was wet the whole time, forty-eight hours; but I warded off the effects by helping the canoe-man with a paddle the entire way, by which means we also arrived at Lagos earlier. One more unpleasant incident, and I shall relieve the reader. It seemed that the canoe in which we travelled was purchased from an Ijebu, and not paid for. When two thirds down the river, the canoe-man stopped at a small market-village, not expecting to meet there his creditor, but did unfortunately. Some altercation ensued,

6*

when the Ijebu began to take the things out of the boat, in order to repossess himself of his property. I remained quiet until he attempted to remove my things, when I interposed. He turned from me, and began to talk very angrily with the canoe-man. Both became more and more excited. At this time another canoe with several men and women came up, and all these took part in the row, which grew more fierce every instant. I saw some of the crowd running away, who in a few moments returned, and with them about thirty men, all armed with knives, their chief at their head. They rushed at the poor man, and the chief seizing the resistless creature was about to slay him, when a woman heroically threw herself in the way of the weapon, and saved him. The row continued fully an hour longer, and terminated at last only from the sheer exhaustion of all concerned. Without an interpreter, and my own knowledge of the language being very limited, I was unable except by conjecture and an expression understood here and there, to learn the details of the dispute.

We arrived at Lagos on the evening of the 7th of April. Dr. Delany accomplished his overland journey in the same time, so that we met crossing the bay, and landed together. The next day, Sunday—

Easter Sunday—we attended divine service, and heard a sermon from our venerable friend the Rev. Samuel Crowther, who was now spending a short time with his family, and expecting to return to his labors up the Niger in a few days. Let me here, as well for my colleague as myself, record my acknowledgments and thanks to him, his family, and to the many kind friends we met with in our travels, not omitting our friend Capt. Davis, who kindly furnished us a passage in his boat to the steamer, free of expense.

On the morning of the 10th of April we bade adieu to Lagos, and after an unusually fine passage across the bar, embarked on board the Royal Mail S. S. "Athenian," Capt. Laurie, for Liverpool. The steamer, as in the outward voyage, stopped at the intermediate places on the coast, and at Teneriffe and Madeira. She had on board a large number of Kru men, returning from different points of the coast, where they had been serving either on board men-of-war or trading vessels. These men are of incalculable advantage, as without them it would be impossible to work the ships, European sailors being unfit to labor in such warm latitudes, and not understanding so well the management of boats in heavy surfs. No where, I believe, can people be found so at home in the water. At Cape Palmas and other places on the Liberian coast, the steamer stops to allow them to land, which they do in very small canoes, brought off from the beach by their countrymen, in which no other human beings would venture. They make a fearful noise as they are departing and preparing to do so, and if not hurried off by the officers, would detain the vessel much longer than necessary. Sometimes the steamer starts before they have all left, and then without the slightest hesitation they throw into the water such of their property as will float, taking the rest in their hands, and jumping overboard swim with the greatest ease to their canoes. Such a scene occurred in our ship. Those who were still on board when the steamer started, had a number of swords, iron pots, pistols, kegs of powder, etc., the wages of their labor, which they prefer rather in goods than in money. I saw several jump into the water with swords in both hands, but there was one who had five swords and two iron pots, certainly not weighing less than thirty-five or forty pounds. Their canoes often upset, but this they consider quite a matter of course; a dexterous jerk from one side rights them again, and in another instant they are in their place bailing out the water.

At Freetown, Sierra Leone, we saw a large slaver, brought in a few days before by H. M. S. S. "Triton." Her officers and crew, consisting of over thirty persons, were there set at liberty, to be disposed of by the Spanish Consul as distressed seamen. They were as such forwarded in the same ship with us to Teneriffe. No wonder that the slave-trade should be so difficult to suppress, when no punishment awaits such wretches as these. What scamp would fear to embark in such an enterprise, if only assured that there was no personal risk—that he has only to destroy the ship's flag and papers on the approach of a cruiser, not only to shield himself and his crew from the consequence of his crime, but to receive the consideration rightly accorded distressed honest men. These villains, of course return to Havana or the United States, procure a new ship, and again pursue the wicked purpose which their previous experience enables them to accomplish with all the more impunity.

The incidents of a voyage to England under every variety of circumstance, have been so often described, that I shall both save myself the trouble of writing, and you, dear reader, the tedium of perusing them.

CHAPTER XI

CONCLUSION.

Willingness of Natives to receive Settlers—Comparative Healthiness of Coast and Interior—Expense of Voyage—Protection—How to procure Land—Commercial and Agricultural Prospects—Time of arriving at Lagos—The Bar—Extent of Self-Government—Climate—African Fever and Treatment—Cotton Trade—Domestic Animals—Agricultural Products—Minerals—Timber—Water—African Industry—Expense of Labor—Our Treaty—*Finis*.

THE native authorities, every where from Lagos to Ilorin, are willing to receive civilized people among them as settlers. It is hardly fair to say merely that they are willing; they hail the event with joy. They know and appreciate the blessings which must accrue to them by such accessions. They would, however, be opposed to independent colonies, the establishment of which among them, not only on this account, would be highly inexpedient.

The sea-coast, from the prevalence of mangrove-swamps, is unhealthy, but it is a fact that many persons, even Europeans and Americans, enjoy good health there, and many of the deaths are more to be attributed to alcoholic indulgence than to the character of the location. Abbeokuta, and all other interior towns we visited, are healthy, but even in these an occasional attack of bilious fever must be expected for a year or two, or until the process of acclimature is completed. Emigrants should remember that in new countries it is always necessary to exercise great watchfulness and discretion.

The expense of a voyage to Lagos directly from America, should not exceed $100 for first-class, and $60 for second-class: via Liverpool, besides the expense of the voyage thither, it would cost $200 for first-class, and $150 for second-class: $25 should include all expense of landing at Lagos, and of the journey to Abbeokuta.

The best protection on which a settler should rely in Africa, is that which all men are disposed to afford a good and honest man. The proper kind of emigrants want no protection among the natives of the Egba and Yoruba countries. We have had, however, from Lord Malmesbury, late Foreign Secretary in the British Cabinet, a letter to the Consul at Lagos, by which the protection of that functionary, as far as he can afford it, is secured for settlers.

Although land for agricultural purposes may be obtained, as much as can be used, "without money and without price," yet town-lots will cost from $2 to $50 and even $100. Some fine fellows may get a very suitable lot for a trifle, or even for nothing; much depends upon the person.

The commercial and agricultural prospects are excellent, but there is much room for enterprise and energy. There is a decided demand for intelligent colored Americans, but it must be observed that one who is only prepared to roll barrels would have to compete with the natives under great disadvantages. Agriculturists, mechanics, and capitalists, with suitable religious and secular teachers, are most required.

Emigrants should never leave the States so as to arrive at Lagos in the months of June, July or August: the bar is then bad, and there is great risk to person and property in landing at such season. For safety I might include the last of May and first of September. During all the rest of the year there is no danger. The difficulties of the bar are not, however, insuperable; small vessels can always easily sail over it into the fine bay within, where they can load or unload with little trouble and without risk. It is not so easy to go out again, however, for then it would be necessary to "beat" against the wind, but a small steamboat could at once take them out in tow with perfect safety. I was informed that slavers used always to enter the bay : they could, of course, afford to wait for a favorable wind with which to get out.

Emigrants going to Abbeokuta, according to the second article of our treaty, will be permitted the privilege of self-government, but this can only be municipal, and affecting too only themselves. There is no doubt, however, that in time it will assume all the functions of a national government, for the people are fast progressing in civilization, and the existing laws, which from their nature apply only to heathens, would be found inadequate for them. Even now, as soon as any one of the people assumes the garb or other characteristics of civilization, they cease to exercise jurisdiction over him. He is thenceforward deemed an "oyibo," or white man.* The rulers, of course, will not be unaffected by those influences which can bring about such changes in their people, and thus they too will find it expedient to modify the laws to meet the emergency. But em-

---

* This term, which literally signifies stripped off, was applied to white men, from the belief that their skin was stripped off. It is now applied indiscriminately to civilized men. To distinguish, however, between black civilized and white civilized men, the terms *dudu* for the former, and *fufu* for the latter, are respectively affixed.

igrants must ever remember that the existing rulers must be respected, for they only are the *bona fide* rulers of the place. The effort should be to lift them up to the proper standard, and not to supersede or crush them. If such a disposition is manifested, then harmony and peace will prevail; I am afraid not, otherwise.

Of course the succession of seasons in northern and southern latitudes below the 24th parallel, does not exist. There are two wet and two dry seasons. The first wet begins about the last of April, and continues until the close of June. The second begins in the last of September, and ceases with the end of October. The period between June and September is not entirely without rain. Both the wet seasons are inaugurated by sharp thunder and lightning, and an occasional shower. The harmattan winds prevail about Christmas time. They are very dry and cold: I have seen at 8 A.M., the thermometer at 54° Fahr., during the prevalence of these winds. The mornings and evenings, however warm the noon might be, are always comfortable. The general range of the temperature is between 74° and 90° Fahr. I have experienced warmer days in New-York and Philadelphia.

With due prudence there is nothing to fear from the African fever, which is simply the bilious fever, arising from marsh miasmata common to other tropical countries, as well as to the southern sections of the United States. I have, myself, experienced the disease, not only in Africa, but in the West-Indies and Central America, and know that in all these places it is identical. Emigrants to the Western States of America suffer severely from typhoid fever, which often renders them powerless for months together; but with the African fever, which is periodical, there is always an intermission of from one to three days between the paroxysms, when the patient is comparatively well. Persons of intemperate habits, however, are generally very seriously affected. I suffered five attacks during my sojourn in Africa. The first, at Lagos, continuing about eight days, was induced by severe physical exertion in the sun. The four other attacks were in the interior. By a prompt application of suitable remedies, neither of them lasted longer than four or five days, and were not severe. The treatment I found most efficacious was, immediately on the appearance of the symptoms, to take two or three anti-bilious pills, composed each of two and a half grains comp. ext. Colocynth, and one fourth grain Podophyllin, (ext. May-apple root.) For the present of a box of these pills I am indebted to Messrs. Bullock & Crenshaw, druggists, Sixth, above Arch street. This treatment always had the effect of greatly prostrating me, but the next day I was better, although weak. I then took three times daily about one grain sulphate of quinine, as much as will lie on a five-cent piece. This quantity in my own case was always sufficient, but it must be observed that the same dose will not answer for every constitution. It should be taken in a little acidulated water, or wine and water. Mr. Edward S. Morris, 916 Arch street, has a preparation which from experience I found better than the pure quinine. The practice of physicking while in health to keep well is very unwise: try to keep off disease by living carefully, and when in spite of this it comes, then physic, but carefully. Many suffer more from medicines than from disease. Quinine should not be taken during the recurrence of the fever. Hard labor or unnecessary walking in the sun must be avoided, but with an umbrella one might go out for an hour or two with impunity in the warmest weather.

Cotton from Abbeokuta has been an article of export to the British market for about eight years. In the first year only 235 pounds could be procured, but from that time, through the efforts of Thomas Clegg, Esq., of Manchester, and several gentlemen connected with the Church Missionary Society, London, the export has more than doubled every year, until, in 1859 the quantity reached about 6000 bales or 720,000 pounds. The plant abounds throughout the entire country, the natives cultivating it for the manufacture of cloths for their own consumption. Its exportation is, therefore, capable of indefinite extension. In the seed it is purchased from the natives at something less than two cents per pound. It is then ginned and pressed by the traders, and shipped to Liverpool, where it realizes better prices than New-Orleans cotton. The gins now in use by the natives affect injuriously the fibre, so as to depreciate it at least two cents per pound. Properly cleaned, it would bring far more than New-Orleans cotton, and even as it is, the value is about four cents more than the East-India product. The plant in Africa being perennial, the expense and trouble of replanting every year, as in this country, is avoided. There are flowers and ripe cotton on the plants at all seasons of the year, although there is a time when the yield is greatest. Free laborers for its cultivation can be employed each for about one half the interest of the cost of a slave at the South per annum, and land at present can be procured for nothing. These are advantages not to be despised.

The domestic animals comprise horses, which are plentiful and cheap; mules and asses at Ilorin; fine cattle, furnishing excellent milk, which can be purchased at about two cents per quart; sheep, not the woolly variety; goats, pigs, dogs, cats, turkeys, ducks, chickens, Guinea-hens, (also wild ones in abundance,) pigeons, etc. Of agricultural products there are cotton, palm-oil, and other oils; Indian-corn, which is now being exported; sweet potatoes, yams, cassava, rice; Guinea-corn, a good substitute for wheat; beans, several varieties; arrow-root, ginger, sugar-cane, groundnuts; onions, as good as can be obtained any where; luscious pine-apples, delectable papaws, unrivalled oranges and bananas, not to mention the locust and other fine varieties of fruit.

Of minerals there is an abundance of the best building granite. I have seen no limestone, but Lagos furnishes, as already observed, an unlimited supply from oyster-shells. Plenty of rich iron-ore, from which the natives extract their own iron.

Of timber there is plenty of the African oak or teak—*roko*, as the natives call it—which is the material commonly used for building. Of course there are other fine varieties of timber. Water is easily procured every where. In the dry season some find it convenient to procure it from wells only a few feet deep, say from three to twelve feet. The Ogun furnishes good water-power; there are also fine brooks which could be so used, but not all the year. The sugar-cane I have seen every where.

There is certainly no more industrious people any where, and I challenge all the world besides to produce a people more so, or capable of as much endurance. Those who believe, among other foolish things, that the Negro is accustomed lazily to spend his time basking in the sunshine, like black-snakes or alligators, should go and see the people they malign. There are, doubtless, among them, as among every other race, not excepting the Anglo-American, indolent people, but this says nothing more against the one than the other. Labor is cheap, but is rising in value from the increased demand for it.

The following is a copy of the treaty we concluded with the native authorities of Abbeokuta:

TREATY.

THIS Treaty made between his Majesty Okukenu, Alake; Somoye, Ibashorun; Sokenu, Ogubonna, and Atambala, on the first part; and Martin Robison Delany and Robert Campbell, of the Niger Valley Exploring Party, Commissioners from the African race of the United States and the Canadas in America, on the second part, covenants:

ARTICLE FIRST.

That the King and Chiefs on their part agree to grant and assign unto the said Commissioners, on behalf of the African race in America, the right and privilege of settling in common with the Egba people, on any part of the territory belonging to Abbeokuta not otherwise occupied.

ARTICLE SECOND.

That all matters requiring legal investigation among the settlers be left to themselves to be disposed of according to their own customs.

ARTICLE THIRD.

That the Commissioners on their part also agree that the settlers shall bring with them, as an equivalent for the privileges above accorded, intelligence, education, a knowledge of the arts and sciences, agriculture, and other mechanical and industrial occupations, which they shall put into immediate operation by improving the lands and in other useful vocations.

ARTICLE FOURTH.

That the laws of the Egba people shall be strictly respected by the settlers; and in all matters in which both parties are concerned, an equal number of commissioners, mutually agreed upon, shall be appointed, who shall have power to settle such matters.

As a pledge of our faith and the sincerity of our hearts, we, each of us, hereunto affix our hands and seals, this twenty-seventh day of December, Anno Domini one thousand eight hundred and fifty-nine.

OKUKENU ×^{his} ALAKE,
mark.

SOMOYE ×^{his} IBASHORUN,
mark.

SOKENU ×^{his} BALAGUN,
mark.

OGUBONNA ×^{his} BALAGUN,
mark.

ATAMBALA, ×^{his} BALAGUN,
mark.

OGUSEYE, ×^{his} ANABA,
mark.

NGTABO ×^{his} BALAGUN OSE,
mark.

OGUDEMU ×^{his} AGE, OKO,
mark.

M. R. DELANY,
ROBERT CAMPBELL.

Witness:
    SAMUEL CROWTHER, Jr.
Attest:
    SAMUEL CROWTHER, Sr.

We landed at Liverpool, Dr. Delany and myself, on the 12th May, 1860, in good health, although we had been to—Africa!

FINIS

www.ingramcontent.com/pod-product-compliance
Lightning Source LLC
Chambersburg PA
CBHW030351170426
43202CB00010B/1339